ESCAPE TO
VIRGINIA

Date: 5/11/16

ESCAPE TO
VIRGINIA

FROM NAZI GERMANY TO THALHIMER'S FARM

ROBERT H. GILLETTE

THE
History
PRESS

Published by The History Press
Charleston, SC 29403
www.historypress.net

Copyright © 2015 by Robert H. Gillette
All rights reserved

First published 2015

Manufactured in the United States

ISBN 978.1.62619.912.5

Library of Congress Control Number: 2015947683

My Hope…
That my granddaughters—
Rachel, Rebecca, Sara and Hannah—
will be inspired by the resilient Hope and Courage of Eva and Töpper
and all who rescued and nurtured their lives.

Robert H. Gillette ("Pop Pop")
June 2015

CONTENTS

Foreword. Those Who Knew Them Best,
  by Jacqueline Jacobsohn and Miriam Angress   9
What Is Creative History?   11
Acknowledgements   13
Introduction   17
About Suffering, Courage and Hope   19

1. Nightmare   21
2. Werner's Interview   33
3. Dr. Curt Bondy and the Opening of Gross Breesen   39
4. Werner Arrives at Gross Breesen, 1936   43
5. Life at Gross Breesen   47
6. Eva's Expulsion, 1936   56
7. Eva at St. Paul's Girls' School, England, 1936   63
8. Summer Vacation, Germany, 1936   71
9. St. Paul's, 1936–1937   75
10. Witness to History   80
11. The Final Push, 1937   84
12. Eva at Gross Breesen, 1937–1938   87
13. "Inside Work"   95
14. Comfort in Routine   102

CONTENTS

15. The Drought   104
16. Heartache and Growing Up   106
17. Töpper, the Spokesman   108
18. A Ray of Hope, 1938   111
19. The Postcard to Töpper   118
20. A Telephone Call to Eva   121
21. Eva's Escape   123
22. "Root Holds" at Hyde Farmlands   132
23. Töpper in Exile   145
24. Krystallnacht, November 9–10, 1938   148
25. Imprisoned in Buchenwald Concentration Camp   156
26. Panic and Response   161
27. Release from Buchenwald   164
28. Thalhimer's Victory!   167
29. Waiting for a Visa   170
30. Töpper's Journey to Hyde Farmlands   173
31. Töpper at Hyde Farmlands, 1939–1940   181
32. Major Construction and a Chicken Industry   189
33. Constant Worry   194
34. Hyde Farmlands Closes, 1941   197
35. "Tom," the War Years   204
36. Eva, the War Years   215
37. Bondy and Thalhimer, the War Years   224
38. "They Who Sow in Tears"   228

Notes   233
Bibliography   241
Index   247
About the Author   251

THOSE WHO KNEW THEM BEST

Eva Jacobsohn Loew

Eva lived her life, every thought, word and endeavor, with one fundamental belief: "Where there is life, there is hope." Deep within lived a gentle, humble courage without measure, from which she met and overcame all trial, navigated loss and sorrow and found goodness to celebrate. Always.

Eva came of age as the promise of her world, as she understood it, was disappearing. Abrupt dismissal from her school and friends, exile from her beloved home and family, final flight from her homeland of which she was so fiercely loyal and devoted. So much, so lost, all at once. Here her profound hope rooted a courage from which she grew and blossomed.

A young life spent packing and unpacking her belongings. What does one bring along when one can take so little? Moving from place to place, forever adapting to new people, countries, cultures and expectations. Always making room in her heart, and every step turned into a place for new opportunity, experience and growth. An unyielding search for knowledge, peace, joy. This is Eva's story. Roll up your sleeves, kneel on her fertile soil, cultivate what is offered here. Her strength, perseverance and integrity will give rise to the best within you. For "where there is hope, there is life." And all things are, indeed, possible.

JACQUELINE JACOBSOHN, Eva's daughter

WERNER T. ANGRESS

If every adult has a period of life that stays particularly alive for them, for our father it was his teenage years, until and after he escaped from the Nazis. He grew in wisdom but kept some of the intense emotion, loneliness and idealism of adolescence. Sometimes he was a hero, risking his life, fighting injustices, battling the Third Reich, and other times he was caught up in his feelings, unable to focus beyond them. Then he'd emerge and be warmly loving and present—a great listener, irreverent and kind.

He learned as a teenager that it's possible to make a difference in the world. Before he was nineteen, he and his friend Meui had managed to get a group released from a concentration camp. He used words to help others, to make sense of his past and to connect with people. He wrote letters and, later, e-mails to friends every day of his life. Making and keeping friends was one of his gifts.

After he retired, he moved back to Berlin and talked to school groups and on the radio about growing up in a context where laws were created specifically to harm certain groups. Even though as a professor he knew their history in detail, he remained bewildered by the Nazis. He described a gentle, goofy relative of his who was gassed in a concentration camp and asked, "How could they hate him?" In his seventies, he bought a book with Adolf Hitler on the cover, and after an afternoon of Adolf's face staring up from the coffee table, he turned the book over. He didn't want Hitler in his living room. Even as a historical expert, he stayed vulnerable to feelings he'd first had decades earlier. But he also taught and mentored many students in German history and wrote memoirs about the first twenty-five years of his life so that others could have access to his experiences. He used his expertise as an act of service for future generations.

MIRIAM ANGRESS, Werner's daughter

WHAT IS CREATIVE HISTORY?

Creative history is history told in a way that reads like fiction. It recounts the true stories of people who actually lived. Often, the real words of the personalities involved are used in the narrative, but in addition, dialogues and descriptions may be created to portray an event, to fill in the gaps. History comes alive in creative history, but it must pass the test of honest scholarship. The enormous primary research required to write creative history is the same as that for writing traditional history.

Escape to Virginia: From Nazi Germany to Thalhimer's Farm is creative history. The stories are true. The diaries, photographs, books, letters and interviews compose the primary materials from which lives were reconstructed into a living testimony.

ACKNOWLEDGEMENTS

It took five years of extensive research to uncover the largely unknown stories and events that were portrayed in my book *The Virginia Plan: William B. Thalhimer and a Rescue from Nazi Germany* (The History Press, 2011.) In *Escape to Virginia: From Nazi Germany to Thalhimer's Farm*, I have traced the lives of two remarkable people: Eva Jacobsohn Loew and Werner T. Angress. In addition to the research amassed for the *Virginia Plan* (for a complete bibliography and acknowledgements, see *The Virginia Plan*), both Eva and Werner and their families entrusted me with their personal diaries, photographic albums, books, letters and honest interviews. Their children—especially Jacqueline Jacobsohn, Percy Angress and Miriam Angress—facilitated my intention to honestly capture the lives of their parents, who died during my research. I am grateful for their contributions to the foreword and their willingness to share materials and memories. The Angress children published *Witness to the Storm*, an extraordinary autobiography originally written in German by their father, now translated into English. Jacqueline Jacobsohn devoted many months with her mother, Eva, translating and transposing her diaries, and she retyped hundreds of her letters. She graciously shared many photographs and artifacts and, through our many conversations, communicated the essence of the soul of her mother.

Abraham Ascher, historian, shared his insights into Breslau in the 1930s. His book, *A Community Under Siege: The Jews of Breslau under Nazism*, helped clarify the historical reality that was so close to Gross Breesen. His sister, Esther Ascher Adler, sent me her poems about her experiencing Krystallnacht in Breslau in 1938 and shared her letter to Martin Gilbert for his book, *Krystallnacht*. Professor Ascher directed me to *No Justice in Germany: The Breslau Diaries 1933–1941* by Willy Cohn. This book personally included the days of Krystallnacht in Breslau and the surrounding towns. Dr. Marcin Wodzinski connected me to Jerzy Kos, of the University of Wroclaw, Poland, who was immensely helpful in finding archival photographs of Breslau and Gellendorf. He traveled to Gross Breesen to photograph the refurbished estate. Howard Bailes, teacher, historian and archivist, sent me his *Once a Paulina: A History of St. Paul's Girls' School* and clarified the historical context of Eva's stay at St. Paul's in London. Steve Strauss shared his insights of the Gross Breesen students and provided photographs that he developed into an exhibit on the student life at Gross Breesen. Robert Flippen, of the Virginia State Parks, provided archival photographs of Crewe, Virginia, from his extensive private photo and postcard collections. Chuck Koutnik, Nottoway County librarian, connected me to helpful local resources. Judy Cohen, director of photographic archives at the United States Holocaust Memorial Museum, was very helpful in accessing photographs from the museum's vast archives. Caroline Waddell Koehler and Christina Berkey, members of the photographic archives team, made my life hassle free.

Banks Smither, my go-to editor at The History Press, supported and lobbied for this book to be published, and he was always enthusiastically helpful and sensitive to my goals. Hilary Parrish, my sharp-eyed copy editor, gently and sensitively responded to the manuscript and made cogent suggestions. Everyone at The History Press made my writing project a joy.

My family—David, Michael, Daniel, Jodi and Susan—friends and even strangers off the street listened to stories about Eva,

ACKNOWLEDGEMENTS

Werner, Curt Bondy and William B. Thalhimer for years. I thank them for their patience and support.

As with *The Virginia Plan*, my wife, Marsha, for nine years of research, was excited to discover with me the stories of those from Gross Breesen. She responded to my writing with meaningful suggestions, accompanied me on book talks and research trips and formatted the manuscript, readying it for publication. She was deeply moved by the lives of the Gross Breesen students. She has always been my greatest cheerleader.

And finally, thanks to my collie grand-dog, Sophie, who waited patiently for her play time as I sat at my computer.

INTRODUCTION

There is a crack, a crack in everything
That's how the light gets in.
—from "Anthem" by Leonard Cohen

In *The Virginia Plan: William B. Thalhimer and a Rescue from Nazi Germany* (The History Press, 2011), I narrated the successful rescue of German Jewish teenagers by the courageous efforts of William B. Thalhimer. This book, *Escape to Virginia: From Nazi Germany to Thalhimer's Farm*, traces the lives of two of those rescued young people who made it to Thalhimer's Burkeville, Virginia farm. Their stories are remarkable. They lived in the 1930s Germany that banished them from adolescence and forced them to grow up before they were ready. Their teenage life was filled with exile and anguish, but they never allowed it to be completely shattered. Through the cracks in adversity, they grasped the light of hope and courage to shape their lives. They learned firsthand what all vintners know: a grapevine that struggles to survive yields the best-quality grapes. Somehow, they survived the emotional torture they suffered during their adolescence. Their lives mirror the lives of countless young German Jews who were caught in the years before the "Final Solution."

INTRODUCTION

They were the lucky ones who endured their childhood, exile, journey to freedom and the final confrontation with the evil that could not destroy their spirit. Their lives have something important to say to today's teenagers who face their own growing up and to adults who are entrusted with nurturing their young lives.

ABOUT SUFFERING, COURAGE AND HOPE

There are all kinds of suffering. Some is physical and can be seen; people can understand it. But suffering can be invisible and quiet, though no less hurtful. It's the kind of pain that lurks deep down and is almost impossible to expose. Everyone suffers in one way or another.

There are all kinds of courage. Some is heroic and easy to spot. But most courage is unseen, residing camouflaged behind uncomplaining smiles and even tears. There are a million kinds of courage belonging to millions of human beings. One never quite knows what is going on inside a person's life that demands courage. Courage is what keeps us going.

There are all kinds of hope. There is unrealistic hope that is nothing more than just fanciful dreaming and wishing. Real hope is more than just being optimistic or looking at the sunny side of life. Real hope is deep and timeless and resilient. It fuels courage and overcomes suffering.

Hope and courage are the right hand and the left hand of the human spirit that keeps suffering people going. They keep all of us going. That is what this book is about.

Chapter 1

NIGHTMARE

In his sleep, he coughed so hard that the gagging woke him with a start. Then he took a deep breath…Silence. The coughing had stopped. The sound of gurgling phlegm rattling deep in his lungs was gone. In that grogginess between deep sleep and sudden wakefulness, he soon realized that he was not really coughing; it was all a dream. Only a dream. He could breathe without coughing. The dream was more than a dream; it was a nightmare.

During the day, bits and pieces began to reproduce themselves into conscious images, as if a complicated puzzle were being reconstructed from jumbled fragments. In it, he sat next to a campfire. He loved campfires. He poked the burning embers that dropped from the bigger logs with the thin stick that he had whittled sharp with his jackknife. He peered into the glimmering coals that shimmered red and orange. Then, a puff of smoke shot out of the fire and whirled around his head. His eyes smarted and he coughed. He turned away from the fire, but the stinging smoke continued to wrap itself around him. He stood up and walked away from the fire to escape the smoke, to breathe the fresh cool air that felt minty on his flushed cheeks. That did not help. The smoke followed him and swirled about him as a white mist. He walked faster away from the campfire where other campers were still sitting. To his surprise, they were not consumed in smoke. Even though he distanced himself from the fire, the smoke followed him, and he could not stop coughing. He broke into a run, but he could not escape the toxic cloud. He felt nauseous. He covered his mouth with his handkerchief, but that did not filter out the suffocating smoke. No matter how far he ran, he could not escape. He gasped for air. That was the nightmare.

Werner Angress was fifteen years old, and he was a German Jew. Often, he found it difficult to tell the difference between his nightmares and his daytime life. Ever since Hitler became the fuhrer in 1933, his life had become more and more complicated and depressing. In March 1936, months before the end of the school year, he dropped out of his German public high school. At first, not going to school was not so traumatic, for after all, he was never a huge fan of school. He found most classes to be boring, and even though he was very smart, he had a difficult time with math and science. He did well in the subjects he loved—literature, history, German and physical education—but only a few of his teachers stimulated him. As with so many really smart kids, if they are not challenged, they tune out and turn off. That was Werner. In his diary, he wrote, "Morning: school boring."[1] This entry appeared over and over again. But he dropped out of high school for another reason. He concluded that there was no point in studying for the final exams. Jews were forbidden to practice any of the professions he was interested in and Jews were no longer admitted to the university, so why study? As far as school was concerned, he was at a dead end. In fact, there were very few Jews still left in the public schools. Most were expelled, and the others, like Werner who were so uncomfortable, decided to leave. He was a proud German, but he was a Jew, and Jews had no place in German schools anymore.

Compared to most other Jewish students, his school experience was not so menacing. One of his teachers once told him that he was lucky "to be in a relatively decent class."[2] If his school experience was "relatively decent," one can only imagine how bad it was for most other Jewish students. The constant Nazi propaganda and the morning exercise of praising Hitler began to eat at Werner. As soon as the teacher entered the room, along with his classmates, he jumped up erectly, raised his arm, pointed his fingers with the rigidity of a sword and saluted with the shout in unison, "Heil Hitler." He joined his classmates when they recited the morning prayer:

FROM NAZI GERMANY TO THALHIMER'S FARM

Dear God, hear our plea,
Let Germany become strong again.
Fill us all with moral energy,
It is the pious who work for the fatherland.
Let good German work succeed
So that we will achieve the Empire anew.
Amen! [3]

Werner interpreted the prayer differently from his classmates. He yearned for the "old" German nation, not the new Nazi one. He was, however, surprised by some of his teachers who did not, as yet, totally follow the Nazi teachers' handbook. To his utter astonishment, he was selected by his physical education teacher to be a team leader and participate in national sport competitions. To be so selected was unimaginable for a Jew. He did well in the competitions, but he was heartbroken when in January 1936, a new law forbade him from wearing the medal he had won, the Reich Youth Sports Badge, because he was a Jew.[4] Other teachers were not so empathetic. They delighted in uttering anti-Semitic slurs every chance they could, and they did not hide their dislike of Werner. In music class, the teacher had the students sing Nazi fighting songs that contained anti-Semitic lyrics. Most of the students had belonged to the Hitler Youth since 1933 so they knew the words by heart. Some would recite despicable anti-Jewish ditties:

Two Jews were once bathing in a river,
Since even pigs sometimes have to bathe.
The first one, he drowned;
The other one, we hope he did, too.[5]

Werner read the newspaper daily, so he was quite aware of what was going on. Ever since 1932, politics had been discussed openly and often at home. More and more, Werner was included in the discussions, and his questions often were pointed and significant. It was in this intense atmosphere that a lifelong passion for history and politics first emerged. He was well aware that the condition of the powerless Jews was worsening. The Hitler jokes his mother told could do little to reassure him: "Do you know what a Hitler herring is, no? Well, you take a Bismarck herring, remove its brain, tear its mouth wide open and there you have your Hitler herring."[6] His parents suggested he attend one of the Jewish schools that tried to replace the public schools, but he balked at the idea. Werner saw himself more as a German than as a Jew; he did not really feel at home in the Jewish world. The Nazis identified him as being Jewish, but deep down, he did not feel that way.

Werner had blond hair and blue eyes. He looked like the perfect, young German, the Aryan face that appeared in Nazi textbooks and magazines. He could have been the poster boy for the Hitler Youth Organization. On the street, people never suspected he was Jewish, but lately, dark, half-mooned circles had begun appearing under his eyes, and the usual sparkle was gone. It was bad enough that he had to face his new life during the daytime. Now, even in sleep, he could not escape that depressing, isolated world as it oozed into the deep cavities of his mind. He dreaded the night and its sleepless tossing and turning.

Werner Angress, age sixteen, was proud to wear his Bund uniform. Germans loved uniforms, but the Nazis eventually banned Jews from wearing them. *Courtesy of the Angress family collection.*

Like so many German boys, Werner romanticized the military. In his fantasies as a youngster, he pictured himself dressed in a perfect uniform with gleaming medals and high, polished boots. He was stirred by military parades and marching bands. He understood why the old

The Nazis stirred German nationalism and pride through numerous marching bands. Most German organizations had bands and uniforms. *Courtesy of USHMM 87891.*

World War I veterans proudly wore their medals on their civilian clothing. Germans glorified the military. Werner's dream to become a soldier was shattered when the Nazi government announced that German young men were to be drafted into the army, but Jews were excluded. This point was driven home when he went to a parade that celebrated the inauguration of the new parliament in 1933. His heart raced with pride as he heard the bands approach, but the song sung by the marchers crushed his mood:

> *Throw them out, the whole Jewish band,*
> *Throw them out of our fatherland.*
> *Send them back to Jerusalem,*
> *But first chop off their legs,*
> *So they won't come back.*
> *Throw them out, all these Jews of Moses,*

Throw them out with their hooked noses.
Send them back to Jerusalem,
So they'll all be together
With their clan of Shem.[7]

Werner could not understand why Jews were not German enough. Hadn't 100,000 Jews proudly served in World War I and 10,000 Jewish soldiers died in combat fighting for the "Faterland"? Germany, as did most European countries, created social and hiking clubs for youth, but by the end of 1933, Jews were no longer allowed in them. The clubs evolved into the Hitler Youth Movement. Its purpose was to prepare teenagers for military service. Both boys and girls were trained in the Nazi way of life. The goal for the boys was to be disciplined soldiers, totally committed to Hitler and the German nation. The ultimate goal for the girls was to give birth to Aryan babies and to support their husbands and the home. By 1934, every Saturday was designated as State Youth Day. The boys (Jungfolk, the Hitler Youth) and the Bund of Deutscher Madel (the League of German Girls) met for Nazi indoctrination and military and physical training. For those not in the Jungfolk, on Saturdays, there were obligatory Nazi indoctrination classes for the "cripples": Jews, non-Aryans, the physically handicapped and other political undesirables. There, Werner had to recite the Confession of Faith: "I believe in the dead who gave their lives for their people. For my god is my people. I believe in Germany."[8] Werner hated attending Saturday classes, but he had no choice.

As Nazi brainwashing through the Hitler Youth program and the schools became more effective, families split apart. Werner lived in a dense Berlin neighborhood. When the days were hot, through the open windows he could hear the arguments between parents and children, more than before. The traditional authority of the papa was challenged by sons and daughters who now proclaimed their allegiance to Hitler's state rather than to parents. What the Nazi youth leader said was more important than what the parents wished. He saw young neighbors spy on members of their own families. Powerless parents began to fear their own children.

Nazi intensive, mandatory indoctrination of youth was Hitler's highest priority. *Courtesy of USHMM 57714.*

Werner depended on his bicycle to spring him free from the dark moods of his home and Berlin neighborhood. When he pedaled out into the rural suburbs, he felt like a bird in flight, the air streaming through his blond hair. When he rode by himself, he never felt alone. Rather, he felt powerful and in control. His legs were strong, and he challenged hills with confidence.

What really saved his sanity at this perilous time was his Jewish Youth Group, the Bund. He was popular with his youth group friends, and he loved to be outdoors, bicycling and hiking, camping and sleeping in tents on the weekends, away from the city and his family. He loved sitting around the campfire singing and laughing at jokes. He had known his Bund buddies ever since Hitler came into power in 1933. He saw them as comrades, more than just friends whom he knew from school. He craved freedom and adventure. When the youth group bicycled into the country to find a suitable camping site, they were always on edge, not wanting to encounter a Nazi youth group that might be camping nearby. This was part of the excitement, a kind of guerrilla warfare without the bullets, but in reality, clashes between the two groups often were bloody. Avoiding a confrontation was serious business, so spies were sent out to reconnoiter.

Except for the security and comradery of his Jewish youth group, everything had changed. Most of the fun in life—and Werner loved to fool around—had vanished under Nazi rule. Outside of the Bund, the easy laugh by which he was known was silenced. At home, he became dark and sullen. More and more, he felt cut off from everything he knew in German life. He felt he did not know who he was anymore. Wasn't he a German? He thought so, but now he was only a Jew living in Germany. After the Nuremberg Laws of 1935, his parents were no longer considered citizens, so that made him a "guest," an alien in his own homeland. He thought about his public school friends and his teachers. They were all gone. They were all silent. They did not ask for him. They turned their backs on him. He felt betrayed. How he yearned for the old days of friends, studies, soccer, hiking and girlfriends. Everything had changed overnight.

He could not understand how easily and quickly so many Germans now worshipped their messiah, the Fuhrer Hitler, who promised them a new life of hope and prosperity. Tens of thousands attended political rallies. At the 1935 Nuremberg rally, fifty-four thousand Hitler Youth paraded before Hitler, who addressed them: "You shall be swift as the greyhound, tough as leather, and hard as Krupp steel."[9] Everywhere, there were Nazi flags and huge banners of red with a white circle that enclosed the black swastika. Drummers thundered in unison and thrilled the people as they have done since ancient armies marched into battle. Thousands of torches illuminated the nighttime rallies that coaxed the shadows of phantoms out of the forest or out of the dark souls of the German people themselves. The blazing torches exaggerated everything, especially the ranting figure of Hitler.

One night, without his parents' permission, Werner bicycled across town and climbed a tree that looked out over the huge city plaza. The wind swayed the branches he stood on, and when he scanned the crowd, he felt he was peering into a long, fun-house mirror of a traveling carnival. Everything seemed distorted. People were twisted out of shape, grotesque in size and form. The torches

Hitler won the hearts and minds of the German people. He often appeared in public, especially at mass rallies. *Courtesy of USHMM 47463.*

cast a supernatural red glow that reflected off the spectators. Hitler's speech lasted for hours, and the listeners seemed drugged and hypnotized. Their bodies leaned against one another. Individuals melded into one gigantic, breathing, swaying organism, a new kind of species that had mutated overnight. The rhythm of Hitler's words stirred the onlookers into a frenzy. Soldiers marched in perfect formation. Brown shirts, gray shirts, black shirts—the soldiers were everywhere. Teenagers, both male and female, proudly wore the uniforms of the *Hitlerjugend* (Hitler Youth). How powerful they felt. How they imagined themselves as brave soldiers of the Reich.

The crowds pushed together and sang and cheered. They were the privileged Aryan race, citizens of the new Germany, soldiers in the Nazi revolution. Patriotic fervor exploded when thousands shouted the unifying mantra, "Heil Hitler." In every city and town, up and down the narrow cobblestone streets, Nazi hatred careened off the old gray-stoned buildings. Werner wanted to strike his ears deaf when the rallies always ended in a repetitive slogan: "Get rid of the Jews!" In the Nazi mind, Jews were not true Germans, not pure Aryans. They corrupted the blood purity of the German race. They were the "other," not like "us." They sucked the blood out of the Germany economy. They were traitors! They were the enemy. That's what so many Germans thought.

No wonder Werner Angress had nightmares. No wonder he felt suffocated. He dreaded every day. His Jewish friends clung to one another for support, but there was no escaping the feeling of drifting, of coming dangerously close to the rocky edge of a sheer cliff. The adult Jewish community tried its best to create schools for the teenagers, but the school rooms were makeshift, and often, the teachers could not respond adequately to the older students who could not understand their own anger, their own sense of desperation and defeat in this new world of whispers.

Nightly, Werner awoke to hear his father pacing. Often, he heard his parents whisper. The whispers between Jewish mothers and fathers, their questions, could not be uttered out loud. The children should not hear them. All Jewish parents asked the same questions: Should they leave Germany? How could they leave their German homes, where some families had lived for hundreds of years? Did they have enough money to leave? And if they stayed, would this Nazi disease burn itself out; would the storm pass? And what to do about the grandparents? Could they start a new life somewhere else? Could they adjust? And finally, with grave hesitation, the most crushing whisper of all: Should the children be sent away, to leave Germany on their own, to have a new life and a new future in safety? These were the questions of desperation whispered after the children supposedly fell asleep. But whispers have a life of their own. Muffled tones could penetrate walls and climb stairs. Nobody was fooling anyone. The children knew. They could hear the whispers, and they were frightened.

When Werner saw Jewish children playing as if nothing was wrong, he was jealous of their innocence. They were too young to understand. The Jewish teenagers were worse off than their younger brothers and sisters. They were caught in the in-between worlds of childhood and adulthood. They knew too much. Many of Werner's friends saw that their fathers were frantic because they had lost their jobs and could not find work. They saw their mothers try to keep their homes sound and safe and normal, but they saw the tears and the fear. Teenagers are often unsure of themselves, in so many ways, but in this Nazi world, life for Jewish teenagers was more complicated than ever. Their adolescence was hemorrhaging.

Werner and his father walked silently on the city sidewalk. His father tugged at his elbow and signaled his son to sit next to him on a park bench. Spring had come, and the buds on the trees had blossomed. Plants flowered and promised the coming of summer. But to Werner, even the blue sky seemed gray, and the warm sun and spring air did not excite his joyless mood.

His father cleared his throat and hesitated. "Werner, there is no future in Germany for you. I don't have to tell you this. Times are very bad, and they are not going to get better. It is hopeless." He paused and again cleared his throat nervously. "I read in the Jewish newspaper about a new program that will train Jewish teenagers to become farmers. I know you never really thought of becoming a farmer—certainly, your mother and I never did—but that might be a way of getting you out of Germany. The Jewish Council hopes that other countries will grant visas to trained farmers. There will be about one hundred teenagers selected for a new agricultural training school, some you might know from the Bund. Are you interested in applying?" Oddly, the silence between the two was not awkward.

Werner quickly realized that his father was deadly serious about his emigrating from Germany. It would mean leaving home and living on a farm for two years and studying to become a farmer. But he would be with some of his friends from the Bund. It would be challenging but fun. His adventurous spirit rapidly shifted into high gear, as if he had pedaled his bicycle up a steep hill and now began to coast down the other side with the wind cooling his sweating face. His heart began to pound with the possibilities. How he loved being away from home on the weekends with his youth group. How he yearned to get away from the arguments he increasingly had with his parents. How he wanted to be part of a group with a purpose.

"Yes!" he said and then followed, "How can I get into this program?" His father responded, "According to the article, you would have to be interviewed and accepted. The competition is going to be very stiff. You will have to meet with the new school's director, Dr. Curt Bondy."

That night, Werner had a new kind of dream, and for the first time in almost a year, there was hope. Maybe he could sleep again, without nightmares.

Chapter 2

WERNER'S INTERVIEW

The application to attend the new agricultural training institute was lengthy. The questions about address and names of parents and schools attended were easy to answer, but the questions that made one think were challenging. The application was completed in Werner's bedroom, where it was quiet, but the prospect of a face-to-face interview with Dr. Bondy was scary. "What if he asks me something I know nothing about? Will he be stern or friendly? Will he like me?" These questions played themselves over and over in his restless mind.

Werner's mother tried to be comforting. "Just be yourself, and you will be fine." These were the words one would expect from a mother, but they really did nothing to build his confidence. His mind always came back to the same question: "What will I do if I don't get accepted?"

A week passed with the tossing and turning of nightly worry. On April 1, the day finally came to meet Dr. Bondy. Werner rode his bike to Kurfurstendamm 200, the street address of the office of the Jewish War Veterans League, stepped down his kickstand and entered the front door. He pulled hard on the heavy wooden door, and to his shock, it glided open with little effort. That was easy, he thought. He walked down the hall, and the highly polished wooden floor tapped loudly from his hard leather heels. The boards were oak, and the highlights of the grain caught his eye. He opened another door, and unexpectedly, it slammed shut by itself as he entered a large room. As the door banged, people at their desks looked up, annoyed. "Be quiet!" shouted an older man with white hair and wire-rimmed spectacles. No one smiled to ease Werner's nervousness. He tiptoed over to a woman sitting at a typewriter and asked where the interviews were being held. She responded, "Sit, and I will tell Dr. Bondy that you are here. What is your name, and when is your interview scheduled?"

While Werner waited, he looked around at the busy office. His father was not invited to accompany him. He would have to sink or swim on his own, on just being who he was. The door opened, and Dr. Bondy, sitting at a large desk, did not even greet him with a "Come in." He merely motioned with his head to enter and reached across the desk to shake Werner's hand without getting up. The office was drab—no decorations, no colorful curtains, not even pictures on the walls. This was a place of pure business; there were no distractions from the task ahead. Bondy opened Werner's stiff folder and read his application and recommendations. He mumbled something under his breath, but Werner could not make it out. Then Herr Dr. Bondy looked up. He said nothing but looked straight into Werner's eyes. The stare was not particularly warm and welcoming, as he hoped it would be, but it was not hostile or threatening either. It seemed to last for an hour. Bondy had a large head and a large nose. He was not so ugly that one could not bear to look at him, but he was not attractive either. Then he began a long series of questions that seemed like verbal pin pricks that tried to penetrate Werner's outer shell. After a while, Werner began to enjoy the thrusts of Bondy's questions and his own parrying and blocking. He enjoyed the probing of his mind, and rather than looking at an interrogator with defensive alarm, he relaxed and even smiled, though Bondy rarely exposed what his emotions were as they dialogued. It was the first time in a very long while that Werner could feel the joy of thinking intensely, of being engaged with an adult who was really listening to his words, really trying to understand him in a deeper way. His words seemed to come smoothly and his ideas were clearly articulated. How much fun to be conversing with someone so intelligent and so focused.

For a moment, a flashback consumed his thoughts. Several years earlier, at the insistence of his parents, Werner had studied Hebrew for his bar mitzvah with an elderly rabbi. One day, the rabbi stopped the chanting lesson abruptly and asked a strange question: "The Torah was created with Black Fire and White Fire. Do you understand what that means?" What an odd thought. Werner was confused. How can anything be created by "black fire"? Fire burns brightly with a yellow-orange flame. Werner was silent. He could

Dr. Curt Bondy interviewed hundreds of teenage candidates for Gross Breesen in early 1936. *Courtesy of the* Circular Letters.

not answer the rabbi's question. Then the rabbi continued, "The Black Fire is the words written on the parchment of the Torah scroll; the White Fire is a special kind of mysterious fire. It is found only in the white blankness in between the lines. That is where all meaning is found. You must listen to its silence. White Fire burns with human questions. Jews ask difficult questions." As Bondy continued to ask questions, Werner began to understand the rabbi's words. Bondy was trying to understand Werner's "white fire," his real values, hopes and dreams. At that moment, something clicked in his mind. Werner knew that he would live a life asking questions: What and Why? And, What does that mean? And, What does that mean to me? These questions would be his constant thinking companions. His mind would never be static. The flickering points of the white flames would forever be darting and dancing. There would always be questions.

Bondy paused, thought and then asked Werner a startling question: "What kind of Jew are you?" Werner was taken aback. That was a question he had not really thought much about. After his bar mitzvah, he never went to Sabbath services, and at home, his family did not light the Friday night candles. He really did not feel Jewish at all. What was Bondy trying to find out about him? What if he didn't like what he had to say about being Jewish? There was an awkward hesitation. Werner was flustered. What if Bondy only wanted young people who were active and committed to Judaism? Bondy was looking down when Werner blurted out his answer: "I'm a White Fire Jew." Bondy's eyes immediately looked up with keen curiosity. Werner explained the White Fire he now understood. Bondy had not smiled during the entire interview, but now he did. His eyes sparkled. Bondy had made a decision. He realized that Werner was very bright and probably strong-willed, even if he really did not know that about himself yet. Bondy had a hunch that he would work hard and commit himself to the welfare of the new community. But he also thought that Werner might be hard to handle at times. The future would prove him right or wrong, but he was ready to take a chance.

After almost an hour of conversation, Bondy wrote something on Werner's application and closed the folder. "Werner, you are quite a mature young man. I like your thinking and your spirit. Thank you for applying."

But Werner did not know if he had been accepted. Within the first few weeks of interviews, over four hundred applicants had been denied acceptance. Waiting to hear from Bondy was maddening, but a few days later, a telephone call from Bondy ignited his spirit: "You have a place at the new school, but remember, it will be hard work." Werner tried to control his response, but his heart raced and he was sure that Bondy could feel his excitement through the telephone. Then Bondy had a question: "Could you be my secretary in the office to help me as I interview more candidates?"

That was so beyond what Werner had hoped for. He was going to be part of the new agricultural institute, and he would also have a job where he would meet the other students. He had had questions that he forgot to ask in the interview, but that did not matter now.

Pervasive Nazi anti-Semitic propaganda depicted the stereotyped Jew especially to brainwash German youth. Notice the hooked nose, obsession with money and Communist connection. *Courtesy of USHMM 25556 (1).*

He was in! He could not wait to tell his parents, who were waiting anxiously. They never expected that Werner would hear of his acceptance so soon. He immediately wanted to tell his girlfriend the exciting news, but then he remembered.

Werner had a special girlfriend. They had known each other all their lives, for they were practically neighbors. She was so full of fun, and she joined Werner on bicycle rides and exploring Berlin. She was pretty and blonde. Werner loved the way her pigtails flew when they rode their bikes. She was smart, played the piano and loved to read books and talk about them. They were often together, but it had all stopped suddenly weeks earlier. She was not Jewish, and Werner was. That was now a problem in Germany, especially because her father was a member of the Nazi Party. The 1935 Nuremberg Laws were clear: no German citizen was allowed to socialize with Jews. The two youngsters were crushed. How could they be separated? It was cruel, but she had to obey her parents. All this passed through Werner's mind as he pedaled across town. He could not see her unless they hid themselves from sight, and that was not easy. With a lump in his throat, he knew that all he could do would be to write her a letter. In a strange way, the thought of not being able to share his good news in person reinforced his eagerness to attend the new school. Life had changed so much in Germany, and he was anxious to find out what his new one would be.

Werner felt he would explode. He had to go for a ride on his bicycle to release some energy. As he headed out of town, he stopped and dropped his foot to balance his bike as he came to a busy street corner. He glanced to his right. A Nazi flag snapped in the breeze. Next to it, pasted on the storefront window was a large blow-up of an anti-Semitic propaganda cartoon. In heavy black lines, the caricature of the hated Jew, with a huge hooked nose, stared at him. The poster startled him. His mood changed from utter joy and excitement to one of hurt and anger. Jews were no longer citizens of Hitler's Germany. Becoming a farmer might be a way out.

Chapter 3

DR. CURT BONDY AND THE OPENING OF GROSS BREESEN

Before Bondy began interviewing students, he had to secure a suitable location for the new school. That was difficult. The government forbade Jews from purchasing land, so the new site had to be a farm that was already owned by Jews. It took several months to locate a farm and also negotiate with the Reichsnährstand, the Nazi department that regulated the entire agricultural economy of Germany. With all the red tape and prohibitions, it was a wonder that the school could ever get started, but it did. With the startling effect of a miracle, a Polish Jewish family came to the rescue. The Rhohr family were Jews who had lived in Germany, but in 1933, they returned to their native country. They leased their estate for use as a school free of charge. The manor was located in the small village of Gross Breesen near the town of Gellendorf, twelve miles north of the large city of Breslau, Germany, not far from the Polish border. The name of the estate was Gross Breesen. It was perfect for the school, even though it needed considerable refurbishing and renovating. The total footprint was 567 acres, with 300 acres of fertile fields devoted to raising crops.

The secret police would oversee the school from afar and stipulate the administrative requirements. They demanded that numerous reports be submitted concerning activities, names of pupils and

The manor house, the "castle," at Gross Breesen, Germany, late 1930s. *Courtesy of the* Circular Letters.

the school's success in arranging for emigration. If any part of the reporting procedure were found faulty, the school could be immediately closed by the police. In a strange way, the Nazis were supportive of the founding of the new Jewish school. In 1936, they wanted to rid the country of Jews as quickly as possible, so if Gross Breesen enabled students to obtain visas to leave Germany, then the Nazi bureaucracy would cooperate with a degree of enthusiasm.

With the school facility secured, Bondy interviewed candidates from morning to night. Applications poured in. Werner collected them and created folders for each one. He had mixed feelings about Herr Dr. Bondy. He liked him and respected him, but at the same time, he feared him. It wasn't that he was terrified of being hurt; it was not that kind of fear. It was just a bit confusing because Bondy could be engaging and aloof almost at the same time. Werner could never completely relax in his presence. He seemed to be the epitome of "tough love." In the interviews, he seldom smiled; he seemed so serious. Werner knew firsthand that being interviewed by him was a grueling experience. Students realized that their futures hung on being accepted into the new school. It was unnerving that

Bondy intimately knew how adolescents thought and felt, especially what they were going through, living in Nazi Germany. By his questions, one realized that he understood their confusion, anger and insecurity. His insight was both comforting and troubling. The students wondered if they were so transparent or if he just had a special way of seeing right through them.

It was now early spring of 1936, and a cut-off date for the selecting of the first class approached rapidly. Bondy, however, had more to do than only select one hundred male and female students, ages fifteen through seventeen. He also had to select and train assistants who would range between ages seventeen and twenty-three.

Parents asked what would happen after the students completed their studies and received an official government certificate of agricultural education. The plan seemed quite straightforward. The students would complete their training, and then they would emigrate together to form colonies in countries that would accept them. They would farm, support themselves and continue to keep their German and Jewish culture. But that was two years down the road, after the coursework was completed and countries were found that would grant visas.

The entire success of developing an agricultural school for Jewish teenagers rested on the shoulders of Curt Bondy. He was forty-two years old when the leaders of the Jewish community selected him to be the headmaster in February 1936. Nazi edict removed all Jewish professors and teachers from the educational system. As a result, Bondy, a Jew, could no longer teach and do research at the University of Gottingen, where he was a full professor of social pedagogy. He was a social and educational psychologist and a brilliant teacher, and he knew how the adolescent mind worked. His experience was not only on the university academic level. He was also a member of a family that dedicated their lives to introducing and developing schools that fostered the progressive approach to teaching and learning. In addition, his background as a psychologist working with incarcerated, delinquent adolescents brought him firsthand experience in thinking about and creating programs that helped teenagers come to terms with their own behavior and their own sense of self-worth.

Bondy was enthusiastic and energized to have the opportunity to develop a learning community of handpicked students. He accepted his appointment with a clear sense of mission. He was fully aware that Jewish adolescents were being robbed of prestigious university educations. He could never replace the academic opportunities that many of the students would have had, but he also knew that the agricultural school had the potential to accomplish what no university ever could: to ready Jewish adolescents for emigration and nurture lifelong values that would fortify them for the difficulties ahead. He was constantly aware that parents had entrusted the safety and welfare of their children into his care. The heavy responsibilities placed on him were massive, but he could not wait to open the school.

Before Gross Breesen opened its doors, it had a clear "Educational Agenda." The "Objective of the College" was to train students so they could gain visas and emigrate from Germany. "The General Educational Principles" defined the pillars the school would stand on. There were six areas: A. Vocational Training; B. Physical Training; C. Intellectual Training; D. Character Training; E. Cultural Training; and F. Jewish Training.[10]

In May 1936, Gross Breesen would soon welcome its new caretakers. The external walls of the manor house warmed from the longer, sun-filled spring days, and the inside rooms seemed to sense the promise of new, youthful life once again. Bondy knew what Gross Breesen could mean to the students. The students yet to arrive might appear quite normal, but underneath their smiles, their adolescent hope had been punctured and their energy oozed out slowly, internally. They felt like their ribcages were being compressed; they could hardly breathe anymore. That's what it felt like to be a Jewish teenager living in Nazi Germany. That's why Gross Breesen was so important.

Chapter 4

WERNER ARRIVES AT GROSS BREESEN, 1936

Werner kissed his mother goodbye at the railroad platform in Berlin. It was the morning of May 9, 1936. As the train pulled out of the station, he waved dutifully. Once out of sight, he was a little surprised by his feeling of relief, not the wrenching sense of separation or pang of anxiety that one would expect. He realized that he was experiencing the same feeling he used to have when he left home for weekend camping trips with the Bund. His youth group activities had prepared him for this important change in his life. Now it was time for independence and adventure, but what did his mother mean when her last words were, "Let's hope"? Was it her hope for her son, or was it that he should have hope? Hope is such a strange word. Behind its letters lurks another word: "Fear."

The train to Breslau was modern and swift. Through the large window, the landscape blurred as it sped by. In his framed vision, the before-place and the after-place were blocked out. All that could be seen was the now-place, but it vanished just as soon as it appeared. Werner's mind wandered in several directions at once. Before one thought was completed, another barged onto the scene and took over. Everything seemed a blur, just like the landscape flying by. The colors seen through the speeding train's picture window washed together, as if brushed water had dissolved the images of an unfinished watercolor painting.

At Breslau, he transferred to an old, slow local train that clunked along noisily. The Gellendorf station, just twelve miles north of Breslau, with its clean wooden platform and varnished interior, looked so provincial: small, deserted, immaculate and yet welcoming. It was the gateway to a village that was sleepy and used to minding its own business. What a contrast to modern and noisy Berlin. To Werner's surprise, no one from Gross Breesen was waiting to pick him up. A letter with the details of travel had been sent, but it must have been lost or overlooked.

Werner stored his bags with the friendly stationmaster and listened intently to his precise walking directions to Gross Breesen. He called it the Schloss, or "castle." Werner began to walk the Gellendorf Road and noticed that it was lined with apple trees whose late spring blossoms still clung to the branches. The walk in the mild spring temperature felt good after sitting for so long, and the country air smelled clean. As he walked, his curiosity was piqued. What did the stationmaster mean when he called the farm a "castle"? It sounded so feudal. After an hour, Werner spotted the pointed high peaks of the castle's roof rising above the tree line. The Gross Breesen compound was nestled in low, rolling hills, none more than a few hundred feet high, and dense forest bordered its open meadows. Winding paths through a park setting led to a tattered sign: "Gross Breesen." Here he saw an ancient windmill and primitive stone and wooden farm buildings huddled in front of a gate that separated the working farm from the main house. There was a stable and a dairy barn, and above them were the homes of the resident tenant laborers. There was nothing glamorous about these disheveled dwellings. The families living in them had no electricity, no heat and no indoor plumbing. For the adults, there was a wooden outhouse, but the children relieved themselves on the dung pile of the dairy, as if they were no better than the cows.[11] These were the signs of poverty and a way of life that stretched backward for hundreds of years. This shocked Werner, and he wondered if he would meet these Aryans and if they would welcome young Jews. What kind of wall would separate the two?

Behind a gate, a driveway opened to a view of the mansion. Werner could hardly believe his eyes. It was a castle! His boyish imagination exploded as he saw knights in armor and horses dressed in colorful saddle blankets clomping on the gravel driveway. This was, indeed, a nobleman's estate. On the surface of an overgrown pond facing the entrance, breeze-swept ripples reflected the angles of the building like light shining off a piece of glass crystal. The manor house was huge, and even though it was rundown, it still was regal. Long strands of woven ivy hung down from outcroppings in the stucco exterior walls. A large, semicircular, enclosed veranda protruded onto the lawn. Instead of open sides, it was constructed out of glass panels that were held together with iron stanchions used in huge stained-glass windows. Werner saw a turret, and he wondered what it would be like to live in it. Finely constructed lampposts that looked like miniature Eiffel Towers illuminated the back lawns. It was easy to see that the Schloss, the castle, needed people to live in it once again, to care for it. It needed cleaning, and a new coat of paint would transform the faded and peeling woodwork around the windows and doors.

His fantasies and personal jubilation were suddenly interrupted by the jarring, stern voice of Dr. Bondy, who opened the front door and walked out onto the porch. He was not smiling. "How did you get here? Why didn't you communicate that you were coming? Where are your bags?"

That first greeting at Gross Breesen was anything but welcoming. Bondy never received the letter that contained the details of Werner's trip, but his abruptness did not upset Werner. It just didn't matter. He was excited to join the small number of students who had already arrived, some of whom he had already met in Berlin at Bondy's office or knew from the Bund. In fact, one old friend bounded down the stairs to welcome him. "Töpper!" he exclaimed. Bondy looked on quizzically. "What is this 'Töpper'?" he asked. Werner laughed and explained. "Werner is my formal name. I used it in school, but everyone calls me Töpper." He continued, "A Töpper is a klutz. A klutz in Yiddish means a very clumsy person. I fall over myself. I bump into walls and break things. That's me. I got that name in the Bund. Even my parents call me Töpper, except when they are angry or very serious with me." Bondy finally smiled. "I guess I will have to call you Töpper from now on."

Chapter 5

LIFE AT GROSS BREESEN

After Bondy's "greeting," Töpper entered the hall, which opened into a large room. He was astonished by the high ceilings, the dark woodwork and the huge windows. He knew that Gross Breesen was large, but this surpassed all expectations. The manor house was, indeed, a schloss. Bondy instructed Töpper to select a mattress from a room used for storage and to place it on the floor in a dormitory. Bunk beds would not arrive until later in the summer. Sleeping on the floor and living out of a suitcase were only temporary, but they provided a reality check. The Spartan conditions reminded the students of why they came to Gross Breesen in the first place: they had to learn to be farmers, which hopefully would lead to their escape from Germany.

The manor house had to be readied as quickly as possible for the students who were arriving every day. Töpper was introduced to Master Carpenter Max Kiwi and his son, Hermann, who were magicians with wood, and under their instruction, the students would become apprentices as they learned construction and woodworking skills on the job. As it was, students learned by doing. They built cabinets, bookcases, tables and stools; refurbished floors and doors; caulked windows; plastered cracks; and painted walls. Sanding, scraping, sawing, hammering, raking, pruning—all were done by hand and took time. The students grew to appreciate the relationship between an object's function and its form. When a project was completed, there was no better feeling of accomplishment for these urban teenagers who had no prior experience of working with their hands. Töpper learned quickly, and he shared in the spirit of teamwork and the joy of doing real work for a real goal. The depression he had experienced at home vanished.

A visitor to the farm noted in a letter he wrote about his impressions of Gross Breesen: "It is gratifying to see how unspoiled and how unsophisticated these boys are. Almost all of the provinces of Germany are represented here; at the table one hears the most varied dialects. The tone is disciplined, but happy and boyish."[12]

New students arrived daily, and those who had been on the farm for a while showed the rookies, called "Ottos," the ropes mixed with some hazing fun.[13]

The Schloss provided the needed space. In the basement, there was a large kitchen, utility rooms, a shower and a laundry room. On the first floor, there were two dining halls, two classrooms, a girls' dormitory and a "silent room" that would serve as a library and a sanctuary for worship. By summer's end, dormitory rooms for boys and girls each held six to twelve students, metal wardrobes, a work table and bunk beds. Bondy's corner suite contained a study and a bedroom, and it had two large windows through which he could observe almost every activity on the farm. The first time Töpper walked past Bondy's room, he did a double-take. Outside his door, there were three traffic lights. Bondy explained the procedure. If the red light was lit, no one should even dare to ring his doorbell. If the orange light was on, that meant that one could enter, but it had better be for a crucial reason. The green light indicated that one could ring the bell and be invited into the room to talk with Herr Bondy. The traffic light system worked very well because there was never any confusion. It protected Bondy's privacy and gave clear guidelines for the students.[14] By midsummer, showers had been installed, replacing those bucket baths Töpper had endured, but only cold showers were allowed, except for a once-a-week hot shower before the beginning of the Sabbath on Friday nights. In truth, the students probably never stayed under the cold water long enough to get clean.

FROM NAZI GERMANY TO THALHIMER'S FARM

By the beginning of August, about fifty boys and girls were already living and working at Gross Breesen. They quickly realized that they were the eclectic few. They adapted to the daily structured routine that started by waking at 5:00 a.m. After a cold shower, breakfast was served at 5:45 a.m. It consisted of hot cereal and a mug of barley coffee, certainly not found in the trendy coffee shops of Berlin. After breakfast, there were classes in agricultural theory taught by Mr. Scheier that consisted of animal husbandry, crop rotation, the use of fertilizers and manure and the different growing cycles of cereals, fruits, grasses and vegetables.[15] Scheier strove to go beyond the basics. He wanted the students to acquire a feel for the wonders of nature and farming. He taught his students to distinguish rye from barley, winter wheat from summer wheat, sugar beets from turnips. He demonstrated how to use a hay fork efficiently, how to fluff up the hay to aerate it and how to load it onto a wagon. There were lessons on how to hoe and weed a garden.

Mrs. Scheier taught the girls. As the boys learned how to farm outside, the girls learned how to keep the farm running from the inside. They learned skills related to the laundry, mending clothing, bread baking, cooking and house cleaning. Preparing meals for such large groups and utilizing gigantic pots and stoves demanded a new sense of kitchen management and meal planning. Each meal became a logistical challenge. In addition to all the activities related to keeping the manor house functioning, the girls learned about light truck farming, and some girls volunteered to learn dairying. Every one of these skills would become the backbone of any farming success in the future.

After early morning classes, at 7:50 a.m. the boys and girls lined up outside in formation. There were two lines, with the tallest on the right and the shorter ones on the left. The girls stood in the second row to the far left, not so subtly indicating their status. This was the German way, and even though Gross Breesen was a school for Jews, the old-world, German culture pervaded everything. The girls accepted their roles, but they knew that they were respected and highly regarded. Being outnumbered three to one, however, had its benefits. What teenage girl would not like the odds? The students stood at attention and were inspected by Dr. Bondy. He had been

At the morning roll call, students received their work assignments at Gross Breesen, 1936. *Courtesy of the* Circular Letters.

a sergeant in the German army in World War I, and his military discipline lurked deep in his bones. After the roll call of the students, Mr. Scheier, as the manager of the farm, barked out the assignments for the day and designated the workstations.[16]

THE FIRST HAY HARVEST

The first real agricultural activity of the neophyte farmers was the harvesting of the early summer hay crop. Accomplishing as many cuttings in a growing season was crucial to ensure an ample supply of hay for the dairy cows over the winter. The initial instruction by Scheier and the other assistant instructors was now tested in the field, and what seemed easy in the classroom proved to be more difficult than anticipated. Dressed in denim overalls and brown Wellington leather boots, the boys soon realized that it took practice to master the skills of using a scythe and sickle and regularly sharpening their blades with a stone. Teenage boys are impatient. They believe that brawn can outsmart technique. Their mindset: the harder and faster one works, the better. Not so. Technique always wins out in the end. Only experience can teach this important lesson, and the boys learned it the hard way. Haying was dirty and sweaty work as their long-handled pitchforks lifted, turned and bundled the cut grass before it was flung onto the hay wagons. The exhausted boys suffered from aching muscles and blistered hands; work gloves were not allowed in summer or winter. But they did learn, and they became experts.[17]

Around 10:00 a.m., there was a work break, a "second breakfast" of barley coffee and rye bread and jam, which the girls lugged out in large baskets and covered containers.[18] This was a time of kidding and flirting. Then it was back to work. The hay wagons were pulled by horses to the barns where they were unloaded. Storing the hay in the lofts was dangerous business. Pitchforks flayed, and no one could really see clearly in the swirling fog of hay dust. Töpper recalled later, "We were constantly in danger of stabbing each other with the pitchforks. Nonetheless, this experience developed in us a spirit of belonging and the will to do good work."[19] It was a wonder that no one was impaled by a fork. After the last wagon was unloaded, the boys exploded with the exuberance of experiencing the accomplishment of teamwork. Together, they had completed a man's job, and they had done it well, even though it probably took twice as long. This set the tone and attitude for the years to come.

A visiting observer wrote:

> The spirit pervading the whole life here and which already now, after such a short time, is characteristic of Gross Breesen, cannot be described in a few sentences…everybody realized that it was actually "our" hay, "our" harvest, for which we toiled…I consider this attitude to the work of the people here to be something decisively important…One other thing stands out here, seemingly on a superficiality: The **order** in life here and the **attitude** [emphasis in original] of the people. One has come used to hold punctuality and discipline as self-evident very quickly… Overall, the people here learn to have themselves in their own control—and for later that is of great significance.[20]

The lunchtime siren could not come soon enough. The boys walked to the main house for lunch and sat at the long benches on stools they had made. There were no backs to ease their back strain, and if one slouched, he was reminded to sit up straight. Each table was composed of a dormitory's members, and each competed with strange cheers and antics before the meal. Following lunch, there was a one-hour rest period when the students retreated to their rooms. This was a time of total silence, strictly enforced. No one balked at this daily ritual that often included a short nap, a delicious luxury in a day of extreme physical exertion.

During this cessation from work, the entire community took in a deep breath together, held it and exhaled in relaxed relief. One could almost hear the castle breathing a giant breath. This was when Töpper thought of how his life had changed. When he left high school, he felt bored, cut off from many of his friends and with no sense of where he was going. He craved meaningful goals, something to hold onto. He remembered the nightmares that had plagued him. Here, at Gross Breesen, his uncertainties were quieted, at least for the present. Better than the weekend outings and meetings of the Bund, now he was with his friends every day, all day and night. When he closed his eyes, his mind flashed pictures of his breaking up clumps of moist soil with his hands. In Berlin, he never planted anything and hardly noticed the change of seasons. He never wondered if there would be enough rain or too much. He never learned to observe nature's clock. Now, even though he could not explain it, he felt humbled and hopeful. Crops would spring from seeds, and he knew he had something to do with it. This was a new kind of living, and it felt good. But, no matter, looming in the distance over Gross Breesen was the dark cloud of Nazi Germany. Gross Breesen was a reprieve, and the students knew they had to emigrate.

Like everyone else, Curt Bondy rested after lunch. His attention never strayed from the welfare of his students and the prospects of escaping Nazi Germany. The responsibility and promises he had made to the parents to keep their children safe weighed on his mind.

AUTUMN AND WINTER HARVESTS

Each day, completed farm chores added up. Just as an athlete trains over a period of time and builds up individual strength, so the students' skills, achievements and pride in their work accumulated. The autumn harvest seemed endless. First, the grains had to be harvested and stored. Next, potatoes, beets and turnips needed to be unearthed, picked up and stored before the first killer frost. That required hours of bending over with hoes and placing the vegetables, one at a time, into metal mesh baskets that resembled woven wicker. The boys and girls worked no matter what the weather. As autumn moved into early winter, the wind and rain chilled them to the bone. Nothing could block the wind in the open fields, and their cold bare hands turned red and became chapped. The days were long and the work was demanding, and there always was a time factor: crops had to be harvested quickly or they would be ruined. This pressure motivated the students and heightened their commitment. "When the last load was brought in, the event was accompanied by shouting, singing, and a general feeling of accomplishment."[21] The ingathering of crops, however, was not the end of working in the fields before winter set in. The students formed a long line at one end of a field to the other and proceeded to move together as they picked up stones and deposited them into metal baskets. From a distance, one could imagine the long line to be the phalanx of an advancing Roman army. They were already planning the spring planting, and removing stones would make that easier.

SPECIAL ASSIGNMENTS

Only two assignments broke with the daily schedule. Those assigned to the dairy rotation woke up at 4:00 a.m., and those priming the Lanz Bulldog tractor woke at 3:30 a.m.

The Dairy

Dairy duty for "cowboys," and some "cowgirls," who volunteered was the smelliest, dirtiest job on the farm. It lasted for six weeks. During that time, everyone knew who was working in the dairy, for no matter how one scrubbed in the shower, the stench of cow dung permeated clothing, skin and hair. In fact, the dairy workers were not allowed to sit next to the others during meals. Even though the students tried to clean them, the cows lived in filth. They slept on straw that was full of dung. Every day, the students brushed and cleaned the eighty cows, but it was a futile job. Everything stunk. Even the udder cleansing solution, made from the residue of potato alcohol, smelled horribly.

The students soon realized that milking each cow by hand was an art, and it required practice and a bit of courage. Töpper was assigned to dairy duty, but his six cows distrusted him from the very beginning. They probably sensed his own hesitancy. Often, he fell off the low, three-legged stool, and one day, just when he had filled a bucket with warm milk, the cow kicked it over, seemingly just to harass him. When this happened, the metal bucket clanged like a bell as it flew against the stall, and the *ober*—the Aryan dairy manager who really thought that Töpper was "useless"—came running and screaming. Töpper failed milking class, and the ober kicked him out of the barn after an argument. Bondy was none too happy with Töpper, but the cows probably sighed with relief.[22]

The Lanz Bulldog

The second most difficult duty was preparing the Lanz Bulldog tractor for the day's work. It was a scary job, for the tractor loomed as more than just a machine. After its fuel was heated by a blowtorch, it mutated into a dragon that disgorged black puffs of smoke from its smokestack and roared in staccato blasts when its engine tried to ignite. The tractor was used for all sorts of chores on the farm, but the most dramatic one was when a long leather belt was connected from it to a thresher. Just positioning the heavy belt required two men. The thresher was a contraption with numerous whining belts and clanging metal parts. It shuddered and vibrated so much that one thought the metal arms would tear apart and fly away.

Few students got to drive the tractor. Sitting high on the seat, the driver bounced up and down on its coiled springs. It was like riding a mechanical bucking bull. The huge, metal, spiked wheels resembled the battering rams of a medieval war machine. The vibrations from the engine were transferred to the steering wheel and then pounded all the way up into the driver's armpits. The noise from this agricultural leviathan rang in one's ears for hours. As one can imagine, being selected to drive the tractor was an enormous honor. Schorch, Töpper's friend, was the first student to drive the tractor because he had previous experience working with farm machines, and he was naturally mechanical. He could be trusted. Töpper never drove the Lanz.

Chapter 6

EVA'S EXPULSION, 1936

Whenever Eva walked down the tree-lined sidewalk of her neighborhood, she was greeted with smiles and questions about her parents' health and the progress of her backyard vegetable garden and orchard of apple, pear and plum trees. Her responses were always upbeat as her dark eyes sparkled with a joyful confidence. Her eyes, framed by her metal-rimmed glasses, were what people remembered most about Eva. They revealed all that thinking and emotional stuff that swirled within her brain and heart. She would not have been a successful poker player. Eva's home was in Marienfelde, a suburb of Berlin, and it served to anchor the neighborhood. Its grayish cement-stucco walls gave an impression to a passerby that whoever lived within was solid and secure. Everyone knew her because her father was Herr Dr. Jacobsohn, who was loved by his patients and neighbors. He always had time, even in the middle of the night, to care for the needs of his patients. If someone could not pay for a visit to his office, he would work something out. Patients would enter the yard past a brown wooden fence and walk on the stone pathway to ring the side doorbell of the small waiting room. After school, Eva, then fifteen years old, served as the receptionist, and when her father was away, she managed the office, especially on the weekends. Often, she assisted her father

Eva's home in Marienfelde, a suburb of Berlin. *Courtesy of the Eva Loew collection.*

by handing him bandages or a patient's file folder. She learned first aid, and a bleeding wound did not frighten her. She beamed when her father talked to her as if she were a doctor already. She loved everything about being a doctor, and from the time she was very young, she knew that she would go to the university to study medicine. After office hours, she often sat in her father's office chair and read a chapter from a medical journal or thumbed through an anatomy book. Everything she read, she remembered. Books and learning were her comfort zone. She never stopped reading, whether it was a novel, a book of poetry or a science textbook.

Her home nurtured her, as did the fertile soil of the backyard garden. Tending to the fruit trees and vegetables calmed her. She learned the art of patience and quiet listening to the earth through all of her senses. She read the cool moisture and texture of the soil as if they were words of a poem or the notes of a melody. She never rushed in the garden and allowed time to vanish into a kind of comforting meditation. She could recognize the tiny changes of seasons before anyone else. She played the piano in the same way. Eva possessed more than fine technique. Because she listened and experienced deeply, she developed an ear that was both a recorder and a computer. She could hear a simple melody or a complicated sonata once and be able to play it from memory. Eva's mind furnished the notes that her fingers responded to. This always amazed accomplished musicians and delighted her friends.

Eva had another side. She was a tomboy, "quite a rough little girl." With her younger brother, Heine, she climbed trees, explored on their bikes and played soccer with the boys on the street. She was "full of pep and mischief."[23] Together, they did some things that their parents described as "crazy." For example, they loved to ride their bikes in the rain and come home soaked or hide in the branches of their trees until dark.[24]

On Fridays in the Jacobsohn household, there was a scurry of purposeful activity in preparation for the Sabbath. The table was set with the best china; the ironed, white-laced tablecloth; and the colorfully embroidered challah cover. The two candlesticks and Papa's Kiddush cup were polished. These cherished, sacred heirlooms were gently placed on the table awaiting the weekly observance. The Shabbat (Sabbath) meal was the time that the family gathered together, every Friday night, but it was always enlarged and enhanced by invited guests. The Shabbat candles were lit and the blessings over the wine and bread were sung. The meal that Eva's mother prepared was always special, but the real nourishment for Eva came from the conversation at the dinner table that often stretched far into the night. She sat on the perimeter of the conversations, but to her, it was as if she were attending the most advanced classes at the university. And they were. The guests were friends of the family, and some were famous, such as Sigmund Freud and Albert Einstein.[25] As one can only imagine, the talk around the Sabbath table often touched on topics of deep personal, philosophical and political searching. There were disagreements among the guests, but there was always civil, patient listening. Eva was thrilled by the quality of the thinking. She wondered if this was what being an adult was like and why her school classes couldn't be as exciting.

Eva was a successful student at her German public school for girls. She excelled in science, and she loved literature. She was enrolled in what would be called advanced placement courses such as physics and calculus. She was a standout field hockey player who played hard and physically. No one could push her around. She was popular and respected by the other girls in her class, but there was a subtle distance between them and her. Maybe this coolness was jealousy or maybe it was Eva's quiet self-confidence, which to young teenagers is sometimes mistaken for arrogance. So often, the life of a more mature teenage girl is a lonely one. She was not consumed with the latest fashion fads, nor did she swoon over handsome movie stars. She practiced classical piano and read constantly. She took her studies seriously; her notebooks were meticulous, her map drawing was precise and her class notes were always up to date. But in 1935, she began to notice something very strange with her report cards. She was an A student, but her grade in German language began to fall. Before, she had been "superior," but now she was just *gut* (good). Of all the subjects, German was always her best, probably because she loved to read and write so much. Certainly, there must have been some mistake.

In hindsight, it became clear to her what was happening. The report card would be used as a weapon, an excuse. In March 1936, she was called down to the office of the headmistress; she was shocked by what she heard: "Eva, you are a substandard student. You are of the inferior race. You are no longer entitled to be in this school. Clean out your locker. Do not come back."[26] Then she was handed a letter of dismissal. Eva was stunned and confused. She started to ask what "substandard" meant in her case because she had been an honors student. She kept all of her report cards; she knew her grades were superior. She could prove that. What did being "of the inferior race" mean? But there was no room for discussion. The headmistress cut her off with a dismissive wave of the back of her hand that pointed to the office door. This militant gesture was totally transparent. And final. No questions were tolerated. Eva stood in silence. The principal glared at her as she stood in front of the portrait of Adolf Hitler hanging on the wall behind her desk. The headmistress did not end the meeting with the customary "Heil Hitler." She would never expect a Jew to respond in the Nazi manner, and in most places, it was forbidden for Jews to do so.

Eva Jacobsohn, age fifteen, was sent to England after being expelled from her German public high school. *Courtesy of the Eva Loew collection.*

That day changed Eva's world forever. She walked to the train station where she commuted to school every day. To her sudden fright, a man spit on her and snarled, "Jew!" First the dismissal from school, and now this. Her world swirled out of control.

She ran home from the station to tell her parents what had happened. She started to explain, but her tears exploded and her sobs did not allow words to form. Her parents hugged her. "I knew this was going to happen, sooner or later," her mother muttered. Dr. Jacobsohn was calm but very serious. The tears in his eyes exposed his fear and his hurt, more for Eva than for himself.

The Germany the family had known and loved had changed in Eva's short lifetime. Her parents were well aware of what was happening to the Jews, but they never really talked openly about the gravity of the situation with their daughter. Most German Jews gathered together in their living rooms to listen to the raving Hitler on their Blaupunkts. The crazed way he shouted "*Juden*" (Jews) was terrifying. His piercing, high-pitched voice rose higher and higher as he grew more agitated. His speeches seethed with the emotion of hatred. They were a kind of verbal fireworks with lulls and then loud, hysterical explosions; they lasted for hours. Jews shuddered, as did other Germans who feared what was happening to their country, but Eva's parents spared her from listening to this self-proclaimed messiah. She had been shielded from the truth. Life had not changed much for her before this terrible day. Everything seemed normal as her father practiced medicine and she went to school. But now, both her mother and father acknowledged that German anti-Semitism plagued the nation and had reached epidemic proportions. They finally realized that Jews in Germany had only two choices: one, have hope that the Nazi government and its policies would vanish with time, or two, leave Germany. The Jewish leaders of Germany and America finally acknowledged the truth: "If the future of adult Jews in Germany is hopeless, what can we say about the future of Jewish children."[27]

Eva's mother spoke softly and without emotion: "It is time to send Eva to England. There is no schooling for her in Germany. It is only going to get worse. She will need English, more than she already knows. She can earn her Matric [her high-honors high school diploma that would ensure her university acceptance] in England." Eva listened with disbelief. Her eyes widened as she stared at her mother. She had questions: Had her parents been planning for this all along? How was it possible to send her to England so quickly, so late in the school year? What she heard struck her a blow so terrible that she only felt numb and nauseous. The thoughts of being by herself in a foreign country with girls she did not know and away from her friends and parents stopped her dead in her tracks. She was terrified; her life was turned upside down. She gaped at her parents, but she knew there was no other choice. Germany had banished her, and her parents had already made up their minds.

Arrangements were made with St. Paul's Girls' School located in the suburbs of London. She would live in a boardinghouse with other students not far from the school so she could walk to classes. But first, she had to pass an entry examination. This added stress she did not need, but indeed, she passed the exam. She wrote in her diary: "Way inside of me, I made sure that I would try very hard to pass the exam. I think also that it was a big surprise and joy for my parents."[28] At home, all was serious preparation for her sudden departure. Eva was terribly upset. She had no illusions. This was not going to be a vacation trip or a dreamed-of adventure, but she had no choice. She had to obey her parents; after all, they were only thinking of her welfare, whether she liked it or not. She barely had enough time to think about this new chapter in her life. Questions hounded her: Would she be accepted by the other girls? Would they laugh at her German accent? Would she make new friends? Would she be able to keep up with her studies that would be taught in English? Would the teachers be understanding and helpful?

For a week, Eva's sleep was terribly fitful. The prospect of the ordeal of such abrupt change in her life wore her down. Sadness replaced the usual joy in her eyes. The greening and flowering of spring held no jubilation as it used to. In her mind, the vibrant colors of the budding trees seemed to be replaced by black, white and gray. That was how she viewed life.

Chapter 7

EVA AT ST. PAUL'S GIRLS' SCHOOL, ENGLAND, 1936

A real faterland you only have once.
—Eva's diary

Day after day, Eva unscrewed the cap of her fountain pen, dipped it into a bottle of black ink and engaged the straight filler lever on the barrel three times. With childish fascination, she waited for the bladder to suck up the ink. She carefully wiped the gold nib with a piece of blotter paper. She performed this exercise as if it were a sacred ritual. Then, with old-world cursive precision, she meticulously recounted each day's activities and thoughts in German. Each entry was expansive, and she always wrote in complete sentences. Even though she was not totally aware of it, through the writing of her diary, she found a way to confront her new life and hopefully filter it for understanding. Her motive was clear; if she could describe it, she could deal with it, endure and try to understand it, a way of freezing the frenzy of uncontrollable events.[29]

In April 1936, just a few weeks after she was expelled from high school, Eva traveled to Holland in order to sail to England. She was not alone; Heine, her younger brother by three years, also was sent to England for schooling, so the two traveled together. Eva

Eva's daily diary at St. Paul's Girls' School in England, 1936–37, became her constant confidante. It reveals her deep loneliness. *Courtesy of Jacqueline Jacobsohn.*

and Heine always had a close relationship, so having him with her softened the reality of being uprooted. It also meant that her attention was deflected from focusing only on herself. She had a family responsibility. From Bristol, the two trained to London, where her brother departed for St. Paul's School for Boys. She then taxied to 57 Brook Green, to Bute House, the boardinghouse that would be her home away from home. St. Paul's Girls' School was not a boarding school, so the dormitory at Bute housed the girls from outside London, with the addition of foreign students from Germany, France, Palestine, India, Ireland, Australia and New Zealand. As soon as she arrived, Eva met Miss Janet Cunningham, Bute House's first and only housemistress.[30] As Eva entered this mansion that was once a huge estate, she no doubt raised her eyebrows as she studied the large pair of ancient Irish elk antlers mounted above the mantel. She was always curious about architecture and the history of buildings, so she was pleased to listen to Miss Cunningham lead a house tour that combined practical information with a bit of school history. Much to Eva's delight and relief, Miss Cunningham walked outside to point out the backyard garden and orchard. It was only a remnant of the original estate, but it was impressive and showed signs of being cared for and appreciated by the girls. In fact, gardening was a significant part of the tradition of the Paulinas (the name given to the girls who attended St. Paul's). Eva hoped she could spend much time in the garden, and she could not wait to sink her fingers into the soft black soil. Miss Cunningham explained that the girls were divided into juniors and seniors. The older senior girls had more freedom, and they made sure that the younger students understood their place in the pecking order. Seniors had their own doors for entering and exiting their own study lounge and the dining room at Bute. Heaven forbid if a junior used the wrong door. Similarly, the juniors, which Eva was, had their own assigned areas. From the very beginning, Eva wondered, "What a crazy world this is. I would like to know who invented those seniors."[31] The school was only 150 meters down the street, and the seniors could walk alone, but the juniors had to be accompanied by a chaperone. Eva found this to be insulting. "This rule may be good for the little girls, but for the girls of 14–15 years, I find it absurd. In my mind this is an education for irresponsibility."[32] After all, Eva was used to commuting by train to school all by herself. In addition, and quite in contrast to her Berlin home, Bute's accommodations were rather sparse, and the old drafty house never warmed up, especially in the damp and cool climate of England.

The first time Eva walked to the main school building, she was astonished as she stood outside the wrought-iron gate that was attached to two brick columns. The iron fence stretched all along the sidewalk that fronted the school. The sun reflected off the gleaming white marble that contrasted dramatically with the orange bricks. It was a mammoth building making a profound statement of permanence and tradition. Just passing through the front gate seemed to set one off from the rest of all English students. St. Paul's Girls' School was more than just a school; it was an academic community with an eclectic history. Tradition oozed from every tile, corner and doorway. A sense of the past touched every student, as if sprinkled by the holy mist and smoky incense of times long past. Then Eva entered the front corridor. Its floor of patterned black and white marble shined like winter ice. She soon learned that the students called this corridor "The Marble."[33] Eva was impressed. There was a gymnasium, a swimming pool, art and music sections, classrooms, an auditorium and a library that was obviously considered the hub of learning. She loved libraries, so she was excited to anticipate that many hours would be spent there in absolute quiet, a rule strictly observed. How she yearned to quiet the raspy chatter that scratched her conscious mind. She knew that the library would be her special place.

The girls she met at Bute House told her that she would meet the high mistress, Ethel Strudwick, as soon as she entered the school building. Eva was relieved to learn that Strudwick was very popular among the students and teachers. Her laughter and energetic eyes seemed magnified from behind her metal-rimmed glasses. She was loved as a teacher while administering the school at the same time. In this dual role, she never forgot what it was like to teach and be close to her girls. She was liberal, and her sense of a liberal arts education

The imposing entrance to St. Paul's Girls' School. *Courtesy of St. Paul's Girls' School Archives, appearing in* Once a Paulina.

was infused into every activity of the school. The teachers at St. Paul's were young, and they felt supported by their leader. Academically, St. Paul's seemed to be an excellent choice by Eva's parents. They had done their research with diligence and received advice from friends in England. It had the reputation of having very high standards for students and its demanding teachers. It was famous for its music and drama programs, and sports, especially lacrosse, were played seriously. Founded in 1904, it was full of

A sketch of Eva's "place of refuge" at St. Paul's library, by Margaret Sifton. *Courtesy of St. Paul's Girls' School Archives, appearing in* Once a Paulina.

school traditions, some of which Eva found to be quite odd. Rather than just being able to accept and appreciate these traditions, she constantly questioned and compared them to ones she knew from her German school. She just could not let go of Germany.

Two meals—breakfast and dinner—were served at Bute House, while lunch was a community gathering in the school. There, meals were traditionally leisurely, with no resemblance to the noisy cafeteria and twenty-minute fast-food lunches of most American high schools. Food is such a personal thing, so filled with nuances and memories, and in the 1930s, English food had the reputation of being bland and uninteresting. Contrasted with the noon meal, Eva wrote: "The food [at Bute House] is horrible and all the things are very dirty. There is no table cloth. There are those little mats that seem so old they stink...I always wipe my silverware before I eat from it...all the

The highly respected headmistress Miss Strudwick. Portrait by James Gunn. *Courtesy of St. Paul's Girls' School Archives, appearing in* Once a Paulina.

dishes are chipped. I often give my food away because it is disgusting."[34] In Eva's mind, this was not dining. This was just eating to survive. Certainly, no one would starve, but Eva was homesick, and meal time triggered that deeply felt malady.

Right from the beginning, she was painfully lonely. She was a curiosity. Her classmates were not antagonistic, but Eva did not feel any immediate, warm connections. Since it was already May, late in the school year, cliques had long been established, and she soon realized that teenage girls guard their exclusive territory sometimes with subtle ferocity. There was no one with whom she could share her deepest feelings. Miss Cunningham, the director of Bute, seemed stiff and unapproachable. When people on the street heard Eva's heavy German accent, they would tensely smirk and physically retreat. Germans were held with mistrust now that the Nazi Party controlled the German government. Stories of Nazi cruelty and anti-Semitism traveled rapidly across the narrow Channel, and many feared Hitler's military ambitions. In the eyes of the commoner in the street, Eva was a German. They did not know that she was a German Jew, and that made all the difference.

Because everything was taught in English, reading took so much longer. Every day, Eva went to the library to read the *London Times* to expand her vocabulary and to keep up with what was happening in Germany. This was not what most fifteen-year-old girls were doing. Her English classmates found reading poetry very difficult, but for Eva, it was even more of a struggle. Classes and homework consumed her days. She felt like she was always sprinting, straining in order to catch up. The only bright spots in her new life were solitary walks in the beautiful garden at Bute House and playing sports. Eva played the guitar, and she played the piano very well, but when she played the out-of-tune piano at Bute, the chords were painfully grating. For that matter, her whole life in England seemed out of tune and out of focus. Writing in her diary became her daily routine and, in a real sense, her anchor. In addition, she wrote daily letters to her parents, and she excitedly anticipated mail call. Her mother wrote often, but instead of easing her homesickness, each letter only aggravated it. She desperately wanted to return home to Berlin, but she knew that her parents expected her to finish the school year that extended into July. As spring deepened and pried winter's fingers loose, the entire world seemed to lighten up. The thought of summer vacation, only three months away, and her return to her family rescued her from the dark place she was in. Eva masked her constant unhappiness very well. Really, only her diary knew her deep, private pain.

High academic standards, parental pride and high expectations threaded together into a school fabric that was recognized and accepted by every Paulina. But what was expected of Eva was overwhelming. To succeed in a high-powered English-speaking school was asking much. There was individual tutoring, but Eva's tutor did not know German, so she was limited in her ability to help, even though she wanted to. Eva had studied English in her German school, but that did not prepare her for this sudden immersion. There were no ESL (English as a Second Language) classes in those days, so she was on a perpetual treadmill trying to catch up and was hardly ever successful. Added to her stress was the enormous pressure to succeed. Eva's parents were academically sophisticated and very German; they expected their daughter to achieve, no questions asked. No excuses.

What Eva was experiencing was similar to the trauma young people go through when a parent dies. There is a period of shock, followed by numbness, disbelief, grief and anger and then a slow spiraling, an incomplete coming to terms with the reality of it all. Eva was caught in a spiral all her own. In her mind, she was always stretching her arms to the east, reaching for a handhold onto something German, but her fingers could never quite grasp and connect. She felt this even though she knew she would return to Berlin for school break. It could never come soon enough. To be home. To sleep in her own bed. To tend her treasured garden. To eat at the dinner table with her parents. To hear German spoken all around her. To be with friends. Eva desperately missed and loved her "Faterland," and her heart was breaking.

Chapter 8

SUMMER VACATION, GERMANY, 1936

Counting the days until summer vacation from school has been a ritual for all students everywhere. The day-boxes of the monthly calendar are ceremoniously crossed out. The calendar's string of *X*s looks like the notes of a musical score that builds to the crescendo of the last day of school. Eva could not contain her excitement over her return to Germany for the seven-week summer vacation. She wrote, "Now it's only one more night. The next night we will sleep on board [the ship], and the next after that in our own beds in Marienfelde."[35] In South Hampton, she and Heine boarded the launch that took them to the passenger ship *Deutschland*. The ship "lay large and majestic in the water, and her smokestacks were black and white with a red border. On a smaller flag was a swastika, and besides [*sic*] that was the Olympic flag."[36] The Berlin Olympics would be held during the time Eva was at home. Being away from Germany in England shielded her from anti-Jewish activities, so the swastika had not as yet become the feared symbol of brutal anti-Semitism. In fact, for the nine months prior to the Olympic Games, Nazi anti-Semitic activities had been greatly suspended in order to put a "civilized face" on the Hitler government for the many visitors, journalists and government people from across the world who would be attending the games. Eva was unaware that Jews were forbidden to represent Germany in the Olympics, even though some were national and world title holders. Before the German coastline came into view, Eva and her brother saw several German warships. One of the crew pointed them out with obvious pride. His eyes lit up as he shouted, "*Sauber*" (clean and wonderful). When Eva first glimpsed the coast before they entered the harbor of Cuxhaven, she could not hold back her own relief to be back home. On shore, everywhere, there were German and Olympic flags and decorations. The entire country seemed festive and confident. When she walked into her own home, she was astonished. Her mother had redecorated the entire first floor with lively colors and textures. Eva wondered why her mother did this now; what was going through her mother's mind to do this?

Finally, Eva slept in her own bed, played with her dog, spoke only German and picked fruits and vegetables from her garden. All was normal again. One morning, when she went to the garden to pick lettuce, the grass was unusually wet from the evening's dew. She noticed that the front of her shoes turned dark from the wet grass. A scene of many years before flashed through her mind. She was a little girl walking out to the garden. The lawn was wet with the same dew, and she became so enraptured by the glistening grass that she laid down and tried to sink into the soft turf. Her clothes became saturated, and she had a hard time trying to explain to her mother how excited she was to feel like a grass-person.

For most teenagers, reentry into one's home and family is complicated, especially when one has been physically separated for months. Reality often does not live up to expectations on all sides. The partners in the family dance become a bit out of step. In the best of times, there are bound to be some rough edges, some uncomfortable misunderstandings, generally being out of sync. That is natural, but given the realities of being a Jew in Nazi Germany in 1936, everything, from all sides, became more complex and magnified. Eva could not put her finger on the cause of the subtle uneasiness with her family, but it existed.

Soon after her arrival, Eva met with Anni, the leader of her Jewish youth group. She adored and respected Anni because she was so energetic and inspiring to all the girls. It was from Anni that

FROM NAZI GERMANY TO THALHIMER'S FARM

Eva learned about Gross Breesen, the agricultural training institute, its mission and its director, Dr. Curt Bondy. Eva was convinced that she wanted to attend Gross Breesen to be with her friends from the Bund. She wanted to study and learn things that were real, that had purpose. She wanted to be a part of a group that had a goal that would find its way to a new place and a new country. She yearned for the comradery of others who pledged themselves to a cause and a future. She wrote in her diary, "I would very much like to go to this school after I finish in England. The learning instruction lasts two years. I think it would be wonderful to train with people like this. And then together with them, leave to start a new community. That is what I call comradery and being ready."[37]

Eva soon realized that any talk of attending Gross Breesen, if she could be admitted, was not welcomed by her family. She wrote:

> *But here with my parents, I have great trouble whenever I say something about it. I can understand that up to a point, because it's very hard for parents to send their children so far away. But I don't think it is right to say no to begin with. Why after all am I in the Bund if I can't help my comrades with all my strength. Sometimes I could get very angry when I am not allowed to do what I think I am up to doing. Then I feel very useless. I could just cry when my parents don't understand me in these things.*[38]

> *Nobody can really help me except Anni and some of the people of the group. I feel terribly alone and I'm longing for something and don't know what.*[39]

Eva eventually grasped the serious dynamic of her parents' fears. She realized that Gross Breesen would have to wait for a while.

The seven weeks of vacation sped by. The highlight was attending the Olympic Games and feeling the national pride and excitement. She stood on the roadside and watched as the Olympic runners passed the torch as they approached the lighting of the huge ceremonial cauldron that signaled the beginning of the games. Sitting in the stadium, she cheered for the German field hockey team even as it lost 8–1 to British India. She saw black American runners and jumpers dominate the competition. She did not see Hitler's humiliation when Jesse Owens stood tall and accepted gold medals. In Hitler's mind, only white German Aryans could possibly be athletic champions. She traveled freely and did not feel intimidated by Hitler's Germany. She did not know that she was enjoying the brief calm before the storm that was approaching the Jewish community after the summer was over.

The goal and path for the coming year was clearly drawn. She would resume her studies at St. Paul's and hopefully pass the Matric exam. It was reassuring that the academic year would be broken up with vacations back in Germany, but Eva could not totally delude herself with calendar balm. The next academic year was going to be long and terribly lonely. She dreaded her return to England.

Chapter 9

ST. PAUL'S, 1936–1937

The channel crossing from Vlissingen, Holland, was not a smooth one. Passengers were standing on the upper deck when suddenly large swells and wind rocked the boat. Everyone was caught off guard and tightly grabbed the rails; one after another, they vomited over the side. It was a chain reaction. Eva wrote in her diary with dark humor, "The passengers started to feed the fish."[40] The rough seas, however, did not affect Eva and Heine. With fascination, she counted the number of waves that preceded the larger one that crashed against the hull. Rather than chaos, she recognized a rhythm to the storm.

After an exhausting travel day, Eva returned to Bute House and collapsed immediately on her bed. The mattress jackknifed in the middle; that jarred her and reminded her that she was far from home. Before she could fall asleep, she thought about the last few days. There was tension at home. Eva wrote, "Mutti [Mommy] evidently told Ruth [Eva's older sister] to do something. I don't know what the connection was, but all of a sudden Papa said, 'Eva can do something now too. In fact, lately she hasn't done very much.'"[41] She felt blindsided. She wondered why her father was so sarcastic. Her father, usually soft-spoken, was tense and harsh. She did not understand that his lashing out was misplaced. To add to her discomfort, her last Friday night Shabbat meal at home was disappointing. She recalled, "The talk was only about how bad everything was politically. Why does that have to be? Friday night really should be the one night of the week where the whole family comes together to talk about pleasant things. But not to talk about politics and actually about things that nobody really knows anything about."[42] She wondered what her own words meant, "nobody really knows," but she did not take her own question far enough. She did not ask: Knows what? What will happen to the Jews? To Germany? To her family? To herself?

The memory of the last few days at home was vivid. She saw herself walking through the Tiergarten to the zoological garden. It was getting dark, and the "lovebirds" huddled on the park benches. She remembered the young conductor on the bus. How very attractive he was. He had caught her eye, and she was a bit taken aback. She wondered if she was attracted to young men more than before. All she could do was shake her head in puzzlement, but with a telling smile. She proudly fondled her new, eight-bladed jackknife with all its gadgets. Such a perfect going-away present from her friends. They knew her very well, for Eva loved knives and camping equipment. The tense last few days at home had been rescued by Anni. She was sure that it would really be good for Eva to go to Gross Breesen and that, sooner or later, she would get there. In the moments before Eva fell asleep, she thought to herself, "I think I will have a big fight at home, but I'm not going to be easily stopped."[43]

Eva's reentry to St. Paul's for the fall term was not a happy reunion. As before, there was a stark difference between the school day of classes at St. Paul's and the time spent at Bute. At least at school, there was the beautiful, quiet library. She wished she could stay there all day, every day, just reading and listening to the silence. It was as if the quiet walled out the intruders of her new reality. She was enthusiastic about the sports program, and some of her classes were challenging in a way that spurred her curiosity. Eva thought that most of the teachers were friendly, perhaps too much so. She questioned if "a strict teacher is really best for most of these girls. She creates order."[44] Eva's German schooling was the opposite of the free-flowing style of St. Paul's. Even though the teachers were approachable, Eva found that most of the girls were not engaging. When she asked them a question, nobody seemed to give her an answer. She felt invisible. She was so terribly lonely. Her questions haunted her: "Why am I so different from the other English girls?"[45] Why couldn't she make close friends like she had in Germany? The only saving grace was that the Jewish holidays of Rosh Hashanah and Yom Kippur were approaching, and that meant that she would leave school to stay with Frau Sachs, a family friend who owned a boardinghouse. It wasn't that she so looked forward to the synagogue services but that she could escape school. "It will be nice to get out of the daily monotony here. Also, you hear about other things as well. I will fast too. Otherwise, I would become a completely simple-minded imbecile."[46]

The Matric exam loomed above her head like the glisteningly sharp blade of a guillotine. In Germany, the same series of university qualifying exams was called the Arbiter. To Eva, the passing of the Matric exam seemed to be irrelevant, reserved for some other lifetime, in some other world. Didn't her parents realize this? Every time she became depressed, however, the words of one of her Bund friends buoyed her up: "Always keep your head up high, even this year will have an end."[47] This became Eva's mantra, and thoughts about Gross Breesen constantly popped up out of nowhere.

As if dislocation was not bad enough, Eva's self-image began to plummet: "Today, after tea, I ran around the huge lawn area with two other girls. I have to lose some weight. Things can't go on this way. I'm swelling up like a clump of yeast dough. And here it really shows up a lot more because most of the English girls are quite thin."[48] Everything was beginning to pile up. Eva was so uncomfortable. She didn't like her school, her situation, her appearance, herself. She read and reread a poem that seemed to speak to her, tried to rescue her:

> *It's dawn*
> *And the fog is lifting.*
> *The whole world is lying in sunshine,*
> *So it will be for you no matter how big the troubles are.*
> *In life there is dawn.*

Trust in God, and have courage yourself
And after all things will get well.
Don't drown in your own troubles, many others must survive
In worse difficulties.[49]

"Don't drown in your own troubles." How easy that sounded, but it was so hard to do alone. Trying to give herself a pep talk, she copied a quotation in one of her school notebooks: "Nothing is so insignificant, so small that it doesn't have value. Nothing is so large a burden, that it cannot be carried." But did Eva really believe that?

The fall term settled into a rhythm of aching monotony. To an outsider looking in, Eva's life would not appear so bad. There were times when she was accepted and appreciated by the other girls. For instance, her piano playing always drew a circle of admirers, especially when she played Mozart and Beethoven, but what really impressed everyone was that she could play from memory and seamlessly switch from classical to popular tunes. Once, without notice, she was asked to accompany a visiting professional singer. She sight-read the music perfectly, and the soloist remarked, "You really played beautifully, how musical you are." After the concert, she received congratulatory slaps on the back with "jolly good; you are really brilliant."[50] More often, small groups of girls circled her as she led singing on her guitar. In one session, she sang "Little Hans," and when she sang in a very sad way, the girls started to sob. In the end, they thanked her over and over, and one girl broke into cheers. Eva was a little embarrassed because she loved doing this and because it put her in a better mood since most of the songs were in German. For a little while, her singing transported her home, again happy and unburdened. These moments, however, never lasted. On the athletic field, Eva was praised by the players and coaches. She was a strong athlete who played with exceptional physical skill, but again, she could not sustain the positive feelings of accomplishment and acceptance.

LONDON

London offered new experiences. The Royal Opera House in Covent Garden became her favorite music hall. Even the Scottish bagpipes had a new charm. At first, Eva thought that they "sounded very monotone," but she gradually appreciated their "more soulful meaning."[51] But no matter how things seemed to improve, Eva remained terribly unhappy. "When I study, I am distracted, and the loneliness doesn't feel so much. It is so empty inside of me. I am missing a good friend. From the people in Germany, I hear at best once a week. Ah! It is so sad the way people are being torn apart… it is hopeless. I am in a terrible spirit. I could start crying most anytime."[52] Eva was stuck in a downward spiral of dark emotions: "I can sit for a long time and stare at one point and think about nothing. I always try to do something about it, but it doesn't work. If only I had a person here that I could talk to about all the things that bother me. I'm so terribly lonely, and longing even though I'm only fifteen years old to be in Germany and home. Even though they don't like us Jews in Germany, I love the country and the people."[53]

Eva was emotionally paralyzed. She could not adjust and go forward, and she could not go backward. The frequent fog of London clouded her vision of the future, and the wet mist coated her with an indistinct fear. She wished she could have taken to heart Anni's repeated urging: "Have courage, have hope."

Chapter 10

WITNESS TO HISTORY

In her last full term at St. Paul's in 1937, Eva wrote, "All day long it was pretty foggy and cold. At times the fog was so thick that it seemed like you only saw a white wall when you looked out the window. The sun at times looked like a glowing red ball through the fog. It really looked ghostly. I've never seen such a fog like that before. This was a real English fog."[54] Indeed, the future of England was also obscured by blurring fog or, more accurately, war clouds.

Eva attended a concert of Beethoven, Brahms and Debussy. As she left the concert hall, still in the rapture of such superb music, she was rudely thrown back to reality:

> *When [she] got outside, she heard drums and people marching. There was a demonstration of hundreds and hundreds of people that marched through the streets with red flags, singing the Communist song…They were unemployed men and women, and also young boys and girls who had come from all parts of England to march in this parade. They came from Wales and the north and from all over. They had backpacks and blankets packed on their backs, and almost everybody had some sort of red piece of cloth…They were collecting for Spain. The men looked terribly unkempt. They looked dark and menacing in their*

facial expressions. They were unshaven…with glowering faces that partially had the impressions of animals.[55]

Eva thought to herself that she could not imagine what these people were capable of doing if they were provoked. "People like that could destroy a whole culture, in fact a whole nation, with their fanatical ideas provoking others and through that drown out reason. This you can see is happening in Russia and Spain. Everywhere where the Communists have their hand in the game, there are revolutions, shootings, and massacres."[56]

Eva feared the Communists; she learned this in Germany, but she did not fully understand that Hitler and the Nazis used the same fear to gain power and, ultimately, absolute dictatorship. Obviously, she had never witnessed a Nazi demonstration. She did not, as yet, have the insight to realize that the Communist revolutionaries were in many ways no different from the Nazi fascists. The "far Right" and the "far Left" were not so far apart.

The British Empire, the United Kingdom, had to deal with its own unexpected turmoil. King Edward VIII abdicated his throne. As soon as the news broke, Miss Strudwick, the headmistress, called the girls to the auditorium. After the students were assembled, she went to the stage and, with a deathly serious face, said the following words: "Paulinas, I hope that I am going to be the only high Mistress of this school who has to say what I am going to say now. Our Edward VIII has abdicated, and the Duke of York, Albert the First, will be the new King. I hope that girls from other countries in this school, who are guests in our country, will feel for us and help us overcome this event."[57]

Eva had high regard for national traditions. She felt bad for the girls who took the abdication as a personal loss.

The weeks leading up to the coronation of the new king saw a London that was "crazy." Banners and decorations hung everywhere, and "even cars had their own little flags. There were coronation chocolates, tennis rackets, pencils…all blue, white and red. If you wanted to buy a dress, you only get it in these colors: blue, white and red."[58]

The only bit of news that could steal the headlines as the country edged forward toward coronation day and its festivities was the tragedy of the *Hindenburg* dirigible that exploded and crashed in the United States. It was the largest blimp in the world and was the pride of Germany. Over one hundred people were killed.

Even though there was so much excitement in England, Eva could not extricate herself from her own worries. Letters from home, which usually arrived on Saturdays, became erratic. This was alarming. She wrote, "I have no idea what is going on at home. If I don't hear from them by tomorrow, I don't know what I will do. Hopefully, everything is all right."[59] The usual absorption into studies, activities and her own misery of loneliness began to include worry about how safe her family was in Germany. This only added to her feeling of helplessness. For a brief period, however, she allowed herself to be swept up in the excitement of the coronation.

It was 4:00 a.m. when Eva and a classmate, Alix, left to find a spot to view the coronation parade. The subway was already crowded even at that early hour. The two arrived at the Oxford Circus station and made their way into the throng that had gathered. She recounted:

> *After nine hours, we were standing probably in the second row. All around us were people from the East End or real proletarians. I have to say that I'd rather be among the Germans than the English. The Germans have a lot more humor, and would if they had to stay this long, I'm sure, sing one song after the other... Pretty soon a Scottish regiment marched by. I liked the uniforms of the Highlanders very much...Above us there was a loudspeaker, and we listened to parts of the coronation in the Abbey...finally it was three o'clock, and the parade slowly came toward us. In the front rode soldiers from all different types of the British Commonwealth. Arabs, Indians with colorful turbans and big beards, Africans, Negroes, Malaysians. It was a colorful mixture of people. They came partly on foot, partly on horseback, troops with beautiful uniforms. In between were bands on horseback, where the riders held the reins with one hand, and had a trumpet in the other. For saddles they had tiger skins. Especially terrific were the mounted police from Canada. How terrific those guys were sitting in their saddles, their guns almost perpendicular to*

their saddles. They were tanned by the sun and very, very strong figures. Then the Australians with the large feather bushes on their hats…So everything went colorfully by. The horse guards and the regular guards. The tall men with the high hats and a majestic step. Scottish regiments with red kilts. Scottish riders on horseback with coats thrown over their shoulders, bagpipe music and the conductor in front who threw his big staff that he used to conduct with into the air and caught it again, and made all kinds of impossible catches…Then came the first carriages with honored guests from in and outside the country…drivers in uniforms full of gold decorations…an Indian prince and princess, the Queen of Norway. Then, all of a sudden, our Scottish guards stood at attention and presented arms and some of the Royal Family came by. The two little princesses with small crowns on their heads (Margaret and Elizabeth), Queen Mary, Duchess of Kent and Gloucester and then a golden State carriage pulled by eight white horses. The King sat to the right of the Queen, the white cape thrown around his shoulders, scepter and staff in his hand, and a crown on his head. So very sublime and royal! [60]

The entire spectacle made a lasting impression on Eva. Everything seemed like a fairy tale, only more beautiful. "It showed the pomp and the majesty and the richness of a world power." [61]

Chapter 11

THE FINAL PUSH, 1937

During Eva's spring vacation in 1937, Dr. Bondy visited her in her home in order to interview her. Eva's first impression of him matched what everyone else had told her: "What a terrific personality, a very wonderful person."[62] Because she had not passed the Matric, Bondy urged her to return to England in September and retake the examination one last time. This was so much a part of Bondy's attitude—one never gives up until final reality is clear and inevitable. Eva would earn either her regular high school diploma or the honors Matric diploma. Either way, Eva was welcome to join her class at Gross Breesen in October. Bondy won the confidence of her parents, and they now endorsed what he wrote to the parents of teenage girls: "Not often enough can the parents be warned, about their short-sightedness in their policies regarding their daughters' careers. If it is the fate of the predominant section of the Jewish youth in Germany, to build up a new life for themselves abroad, then the girls must not be artificially kept away from a corresponding vocational preparation."[63]

Between the time Hitler took office in 1933 and the opening of the training school in 1936, ninety-five anti-Jewish laws had been enacted that prevented Jews from participating in German life. Eva's parents finally read the handwriting on the wall, and its scrawl was all too

Dr. Bondy interviewed Eva as a candidate for Gross Breesen. The two instantly connected. *Courtesy of the Eva Loew collection.*

clear: there was little hope for a fulfilling life for themselves and their children in Germany. They did not need any more prodding.

Bondy was enthusiastic to have Eva. He recognized in her a never-give-up spirit and her desire to contribute to the community. He loved the fact that she was serious about classical music and literature; that she was a pianist, like himself; and that she dearly wanted to be a farmer. He was confident that she would work harder and learn faster than anyone else and that she would catch up with the other students in no time.

SEPTEMBER 1937

Back at St. Paul's, Eva devoted every minute to studying for the upcoming exam. Others had given up their studying, but Eva crammed to the very last minute.

Only her birthday interrupted her routine. Two presents arrived from home, a book and a first aid kit. Eva wrote, "I was so happy. I think until now, I've never had that much joy about a birthday present. I actually jumped up in the air because I liked it so much… People are really thinking about me."[64]

With the tests over, Eva felt relieved and free. The results of the exam were announced several days later. It is hard to imagine, but Eva missed passing the Matric by only ten points. Out of 130 girls, only 30 passed, and 65 failed completely. Even in mathematics, she scored with an 80 percent. Considering the language barrier, Eva accomplished an extraordinary feat. She did not achieve Matric honors level, but she did earn the "General Schools Level." She knew that her parents would be disappointed, but she had worked so hard and tried her best.

Looking Back at St. Paul's

Eva mused:

> At home at first I'm going to feel funny, when I think that I'll never have to come back here again. Never to see all these girls again which I'm somewhat sorry about, never to have to eat this horrible food, never to have to feel so lonely, and that all this kind of life has no meaning. The year in England is now almost finished, and now it seems to have gone by very fast. Sometimes I actually thought that I couldn't deal with it anymore, but now it seems all like a bad dream. I didn't have much fun here, only study, study and study which was not always satisfying. Sometimes I thought I would go crazy because I was so lonely. Why didn't I find real friends here? Is it my fault? Is there something about me that repels others? I would like to know that.[65]

After what seemed such a long time, Eva no longer felt she was in exile. She was going home; she was going to Gross Breesen.

Chapter 12

EVA AT GROSS BREESEN, 1937–1938

The day before Eva was to leave for Gross Breesen, she had a stressful interaction with her father. The two snapped at each other over nothing. Her father was particularly anxious. He saw Eva's leaving home once again as one step closer to her emigration; one step closer to becoming a farmer, which her parents never imagined; one step closer to losing their daughter to the world. But this time, Eva was not so affected by the tension. After all, she had been on her own in a foreign country for over a year. She was not just a young teenager anymore. She had suffered severe loneliness and anxiety, but she had emerged more mature, tougher and more self-confident. On October 4, 1937, her parents waved goodbye at the Berlin station; they were shaken, but Eva was excited. Finally, after over a year and so many tears, she was about to start her new life.

Just like Töpper on his way to Gross Breesen the year before, Eva peered out the train window. Her thoughts wandered erratically, from visions of England, to home, to the scenes of patchwork farms and tall church steeples of small villages that sped by. Her dark brown eyes radiated excitement. Most often, her eyes were soft and peaceful, inviting relationship, but when pure joy overtook her, they shone brilliantly. She sensed that her joy was more than happiness. It was deeper, overwhelming. That had never happened in England.

The ride from Berlin to Breslau on the express train took about four hours. She had several hours to spare before the departure of the local train to Gellendorf, so, as she often did in London, after storing her bags, she set out to explore the city. Her first impression was one of pleasant shock at how large and beautiful Breslau was. She marveled at the carved stone façades of old buildings, and she did not hesitate to ask a passerby a question about this building or that. She felt like she was already a "world traveler." Here, not like in London, she conversed in her native tongue. How easy that made everything. No one looked at her strangely when she spoke. Breslau was the third-largest city in Germany, and it had a very long and successful Jewish history. In 1937, twenty thousand Jews lived in the city. She walked past the New Synagogue and the White Stork Synagogue, two magnificent structures, and nearby was the famous Jewish Theological Seminary. In her mind, Breslau was a smaller version of Berlin. She was impressed, and she wondered if the students from Gross Breesen ever traveled to Breslau for cultural events, especially concerts, but she did not really know how far away the school was.

The train for Gellendorf left exactly on schedule. Its steam engine chugged along slowly as if out of breath as it crossed the railroad bridge over the Oder River. She looked down and saw barges and boats making their way north and south, picking up coal and grain and depositing manufactured goods. The Oder was the artery that connected all of eastern Germany. As the train proceeded north of Breslau, she saw tidy farms and dense forests. She could not stop smiling. If other passengers studied her, they would have thought her a bit strange. As the train slowed and the brakes squealed to a stop at the Gellendorf station, she saw a young woman waiting on the platform and wondered if she could be from Gross Breesen. She was right. Her name was Trudi, and she would become one of Eva's closest friends. Carrying suitcases, the two walked south on the Gellendorf road that was bordered with apple trees that were laden with fruit. The two girls picked apples for a snack as they made their way. How much sense that made, Eva thought, having fruit trees planted next to a road. The trees are beautiful and they can be harvested easily. Eva was already thinking like a farmer. The two chatted energetically. When she first glimpsed the castle, she could not hold back her exuberance. A tiny squeal escaped from her lips.

Dr. Bondy greeted her warmly, and a student helped with her bag and led her along a hallway. Eva was astonished as she passed through the doorway. The carved woodwork glowed deeply from the many years of polishing. The deeply tooled circular designs reflected highs and lows. She paused to study the craftsmanship. This was an elegance she had not anticipated. The two arrived at her room, and Trudi designated Eva's bunk bed and metal wardrobe. As she looked around, she realized that so much work had been accomplished before she arrived. She felt a little out of place because she was wearing a silk blouse and fashionable shoes and everyone else wore plain work clothes. As was the custom, people dressed up when they traveled on a train, but Eva wondered if the other girls thought she was just another "city girl" who would not fit in, who was afraid to get her hands dirty. As it turned out, there were, in fact, a few girls who were a bit put off by her appearance, but their initial reactions changed quickly. There were ten girls and a leader in Eva's room. Immediately, she found a new friend in Ilse. The girls quickly briefed Eva on who was who and what the activities and schedule were. At dinner, all eyes were on Eva, especially the boys', not just because she was newly arrived but also because she was attractive. There was a song followed by a greeting from Dr. Bondy. Life was certainly going to be so different from Bute House. She had dreamed so often of what Gross Breesen would be like and how the students would behave. This was one time when the dream and the reality seemed the same.

Eva met Mrs. Scheier and learned about the schedule of work activities and classes. On the next day, the girls gathered around a large kitchen table to taste the very first butter they had churned from the milk from the dairy. There was a silent anticipation as one of the girls gave it a taste. "The butter was a little bit soft and not salted enough, but that didn't put a damper on the euphoria. It really tasted wonderful."[66] The girls couldn't wait to serve the luxury to the rest at dinner.

Eva's first tour of duty was the house-cleaning brigade. The work was dusty, and washing the floors on hands and knees was

Eva marveled at the intricate woodwork at Gross Breesen. *Courtesy of Jerzy Kos.*

backbreaking. No matter, she threw herself into the chores and always did more than was expected. If a job needed to be finished, she completed it even if she did it during her free time. Not every girl was like that, but there were enough others who were that she never felt out of place. Within a week, she felt at home, so unlike her experience at St. Paul's.

Eva did not write in her diary every day once she integrated into life at Gross Breesen. She did not have to. In England, her diary was her only confidant, but here, she had opportunities to talk with people she liked and had much in common with. The daily notes that she now kept were related to her studies and work activities.

Housekeeping, laundry, mending, ironing, canning, cooking, tending to the chickens and some truck farming—these activities kept the girls very busy. Eva especially liked baking bread in the outside oven, which involved building the cooking fire. She energetically split the kindling and stacked it neatly. But what caught her curiosity the most was dairying, even though few girls volunteered for dairy work; it was too dirty, and getting up at four o'clock in the morning, day after day, was dreadful.

Eva (middle) learned many household chores at Gross Breesen. Here, the girls intently mend the countless socks. *Courtesy of the Eva Loew collection.*

Bondy always feared that the Gestapo could close down Gross Breesen at any time. Therefore, learning to become efficient farmers had to be accelerated. He realized that Eva would be a great member of an emigration team, so he assigned her to the dairy just a few weeks after she arrived. She was on the "fast track" to qualify for emigration. Eva happily accepted the dairy assignment. Quite honestly, she was excited to be out of the house and working with the cows. In addition, she began to realize that she worked very well with young men. Often, she found it easier to be with them rather than with girls. Boys were not so chatty, and she could say exactly what was on her mind without fear of hurting anyone's feelings. From the males' point of view, that was perfectly acceptable, though they were curious as to how she would handle the dairying.

As Töpper had experienced earlier, the *oberschweitzer*, the dairy manager, was a gruff and demanding taskmaster. He considered the eighty cows his own personal property. He was proud that the dairy produced four hundred liters of milk each day. He didn't talk, he yelled. If someone did something that he did not like, his ranting exploded from the barn and loud-speakered throughout the farm. Eva's first day in the dairy was memorable. She rose at 4:00 a.m., dressed and sipped warm tea and walked to the barn. The stables were ancient, probably built in the eighteenth century when Gross Breesen was still a nobleman's castle. She was given a pail, a low stool and eight cows to milk. Mimicking the student next to her, she yelled "*uff*" and added an encouraging gentle kick, and after the cow stood up, she sat under her with the pail between her legs, cleaned the cow's udders and began milking. Eva had strong, large, piano-playing hands.[67] She possessed a natural, dairyman's touch, firm but gentle, and right from the beginning, the first cow she milked did not protest. Eva thrilled at the first squirt of steamy milk as it hit the bottom of the pail and made a metallic sound. On the very first day, after the pail was filled halfway, suddenly the cow kicked it over. The ober, who was watching, screamed an insult. Eva did not even flinch, but the cow added insult to injury by swishing her dirty, dung-crusted tail across her face. Not even a protest from Eva escaped her lips.

She learned quickly that hand milking is not a jerking motion. She closed her thumb and index finger around the teat, and then as she squeezed downward, the rest of her hand automatically closed. Each hand worked simultaneously in an alternating rhythm. On one occasion, she failed to clean all the milk out of a pail. The ober saw this, picked up the pail and threw the remaining milk into her face. The boys were flabbergasted that Eva did not burst into tears and run from the barn. In her mind, this behavior was nothing compared to what she had suffered for a year in England. When the ober turned his back and left the barn, Eva burst into uncontrollable, deep laughter. This was the last time the ober yelled at her because she soon proved to be his best student.

No matter how smelly, Eva thought that the best part of working in the dairy was feeding the cute calves. She put her finger into the calf's mouth to encourage her to suck, and she was awe-struck that a baby calf actually sucked on her finger. It was so wet and warm and trusting, even though the calf's tongue was rough as sandpaper. Eva sang German nursery melodies to the calves, just as she sang and whistled continuously when she milked the mature cows.

The dairy students were called the "people on the fringe."[68] That was a nice way of saying that they needed to stay clear of everyone else because they stank. Eva thought it was all part of the experience, and she was up for the challenge. The currying and brushing to clean the cows was enjoyable when she saw the coats shine, even though she knew they would get dirty again overnight. At first, Eva's hands suffered hand cramps from milking, so much so that she could barely open or close her fingers. In addition, her hands blistered from shoveling manure. All that did not matter. She often listened

The dairy crew at Gross Breesen. Eva (front row, second from the left) fit right in. Notice her leather work boots. *Courtesy of the Eva Loew collection.*

quietly to the heavy breathing of the cows and warmed her chapped hands on their flanks. Admittedly, the hardest part of working in the dairy was getting up so early, but all that was inconsequential because the people she worked with became such good friends, some for a lifetime.[69]

Besides the dairy, Eva looked forward to working in the small vegetable gardens, just as she did in her own backyard in Berlin and at Bute House. Even though she felt competent, she welcomed expanding her knowledge. She took copious notes and kept a work diary. She just loved the feeling of being productive, and the rhythm and routine of the work soothed her. She adored her cows and their calves, but she was also excited to carry the newly hatched chicks into the warm kitchen to escape the night chill.[70] Eva was endowed with special sensory receptors that captured the life-pulses of animals and growing vegetables. It all thrilled her. She felt so alive and so hopeful. Now, when she played the grand piano with her rough farmer's hands, the music seemed even more beautiful. The notes became bolder and more expressive.

Eva was a joyful young woman. Gross Breesen turned out to be exactly what she yearned for and needed. It gave her the opportunity to discover who she truly was. She often wondered where she would be if it were not for Gross Breesen. It came at a critical time in her life.

Chapter 13

"INSIDE WORK"

LIFE LESSONS

Most workdays were spent outside. That's where farming takes place, but there was another kind of farming that needed to be accomplished. Just as there is exterior weather—clouds, sun, wind and rain—so there is interior weather: what's going on inside a person's mind and heart. That was the weather that concerned Curt Bondy the most, the weather of a person's character. As the months progressed, the lessons of farming were learned by necessity, repetition and experience, but the life lessons that would become the backbone for survival had to be learned and practiced until they became part of every student's instinctual behavior. The students were studying agriculture because they were to become farmers in countries outside Germany. It was a ticket to safety. Their parents feared that their children would become merely farmhands or peasants. To the contrary, Bondy saw the students as "settlers" who were educated, self-educating, moral and cultured.[71] For adolescents, life is in the here and now. The future is some far-off place. Not so in Bondy's view. He knew what was in store for his students when they emigrated from Germany. He knew that wherever that place might be, it would be startling, blinding and confusing. Emigrating from

Germany would be like traveling into a new time warp, and he did not have much time to prepare the students for the new life that was brinking closer and closer. Their journey would demand strengths of personality: courage, hope and genuine self-confidence. But how does one teach this? How does one help teenagers grow up even before they are ready? How could Bondy fortify his students against what was looming on the horizon?

At one of his weekly *lebenskunde* ("insights into living") talks, Bondy addressed the students by stating that Gross Breesen was *not* a Kafka "Schloss." The students looked at one another in puzzlement. What did he mean? Only some of the older counselors nodded and smiled. They understood what Bondy was referring to. Franz Kafka was a great writer who wrote a book entitled *The Castle*. In the story, there was a castle that resembled the manor house of Gross Breesen. All the townspeople believed that inside the castle was abundant magnificence; they spent their entire lives yearning to be invited to enter its regal halls. In reality, they did not know that the castle was only an illusion. There was nothing inside. It was empty. The castle was really a reflection of the misguided townsfolk.

Bondy's Schloss was not like Kafka's. His was filled with life and meaning. He wanted his castle to be filled with young people who possessed "attentiveness" and self-understanding. During one life lesson talk, he stated:

> *Mr. Scheier told you to keep your eyes open in order to become accustomed to everything that is going on in nature. "You must observe" was his constant warning. My demand is that you shall live with self-awareness. You shall learn to recognize yourselves with your inner eye, you shall know what you are doing and why you are doing it. You shall not become farm workers, but settlers who can manage and make decisions self-confidently. I demand that you be ambitious and live a life with a meaning to it.*[72]

Bondy squeezed meaning out of every experience that the students had during the week. He saw the possibilities for new self-awareness through incidents that actually happened. He often worked out in the fields with the students and recorded in his mind what the students were doing and saying. These became teachable moments that were gleaned from the students' actual experiences. What someone would think as perfectly mundane, Bondy saw as a self-learning possibility. For example, once there was an argument, and he asked those involved to try to understand why they quarreled and what they learned about themselves in the process. Bondy's construction materials, his building blocks, were personal values, and he hoped they would become as strong and supporting as the heavy beams and cement walls of the Schloss. He pleaded: Live with integrity. Understand your own motives for your actions. Be truthful. Cooperate, commit, think! These were the ideas spoken over and over again until the students grasped their meanings and called them their own. Bondy's urgings became "the still small voice" that echoed in every student. The trust within the community depended on the students' willingness and ability "to scrutinize his or her behavior at all times in order to determine whether it was in accordance with the ethical and moral standards of the Breesen community."[73] The students no longer had a home in Germany; they struggled to understand why they were banished, why their lives no longer counted, but Gross Breesen gave them a new kind of home: being at home with themselves. The students began to believe in themselves and their purpose. They believed they would succeed and survive. They gained hope and courage. Bondy did not treat them as mere teenagers. He spoke with them as if they were adults, and he expected mature behavior. He set the bar high, and the students consciously strove to reach that height.

Bondy came into their lives at just the right time. He was more than a headmaster. He was a disciplinarian, a father figure, an administrator, a teacher, a youth group leader, a coach, a source of outside information, a personal counselor, a trusted friend. His name changed depending on the circumstance. He was Herr Dr. Bondy in very formal times, "the professor" most of the time and "Bo" when intimate feelings were shared. Bo became the most used name. Bo was the name of mutual trust, respect and security.

ACADEMICS

Late in the afternoon and in the evening, there were classes in subjects that cultivated the mind much as the students cultivated the land: geography, mathematics, literature, history, biology, botany, physics, economics and language. These were the subjects that the students missed because they were forbidden to attend the German schools. Extensive note-taking was required, as were quizzes and examinations.[74]

CULTURE

For Bondy, in order to become a well-rounded individual, one needed to be exposed to more than vocational and academic subjects. To him, the arts were what humanized humankind. Töpper and Eva loved words. They both listened intently when Bondy read from German literature, especially from Schiller and Goethe. Lessing's play *Nathan the Wise* was incredibly meaningful and timely when it was performed by the students.[75]

Most of the students had not been previously exposed to classical music, but some were advanced musicians. Every night for ten minutes after supper, a string trio or quartet played classical music, and Bondy or Eva often accompanied the group on the grand piano that was their pride and joy. Eva especially loved the inclusion of serious classical music into the fabric of each day. One night, a large sign was hung in the dining room: "Gala performance of the opera *Carmen* in the great hall." When the students saw the sign, they immediately returned to their rooms and dressed up for the occasion. At dinner, the student waiters dressed as if they were serving in a fine Berlin restaurant, napkin draped over one arm. Bondy was totally into the merriment. Instead of his usual "Sit," he politely requested, "Ladies and gentlemen, please take your seats." A reception followed dinner, and the opera was played on the radio. A visitor observed the incident and wrote, "One saw, in this cheerful, open-

After dinner, daily classical music concerts by the students were woven into the day's routine. *Courtesy of the Angress family collection.*

minded manner, in which all involved themselves in this innocent merriment, how mutually agreed the people in Gross Breesen are. Not only at such happy occasions, one recognizes that Gross Breesen has united these people into a real community."[76]

Bondy and his assistants were not the only teachers. On occasion, guest lecturers met with the students. One such visitor was the famous philosopher Martin Buber, whose topic was "Love your neighbor, for he is like you." Töpper strained to hear every word, though he admitted that most of what Buber talked about sailed over his head. Just having Buber in residence, however, was exciting and to be remembered. It served to reinforce the significance the Jewish community was placing on Gross Breesen.

An Island

Gross Breesen was an island surrounded by the stormy sea of brutal racism. Often, Bondy spoke to the students about the political situation in Germany, but he was careful not to totally scare anyone or paint a picture that was so depressing that it destroyed all hope. Everyone knew how bad things were and became experts in reading between the lines of Bondy's comments. Newspapers were available every day, and the radio, especially from France, painted a bleak future for the Jews and all of Europe.

On occasion, students did leave the grounds and interacted with the people of the small village of Gross Breesen. Töpper drove the wagon to the distillery with a load of potatoes and also with grain to the mill. During these interactions, there were few signs of anti-Semitism. There were no uniformed Nazis parading around in the village. There were no Nazi flags and banners. Farmers were working hard to earn a living, and they respected other farmers who were doing the same. But that did not mean that Nazi control did not enter the castle.

Burning Books

The Nazi order to burn books that were "objectionable" had to be obeyed. Töpper was asked by Bondy to help another Breesener burn certain books in the large furnace in the basement. Fifty books were burned that day. Bondy supervised the selection. To burn great German literature, philosophy and science made him angry and deeply sad.[77] One of the books may well have been *Alamansor*, a play written in 1821 by the German-Jewish poet Heinrich Heine. One of its lines was tragically prophetic: "Where they burn books, so too will they in the end burn human beings." (Heine's play was talking about the burning of the Koran during the Spanish Inquisition.) Töpper's face reflected the red flames as he threw books into the furnace. He sweated profusely, and he began to fully comprehend the full meaning of destroying books written by Jews and other "enemies" of the Nazi state. Before he threw a book into the furnace, he hesitated, read the title out loud and mentioned the author's name. It was as if he were attending a long line of funerals. By the time he finished, he was tearfully, emotionally exhausted.

Chapter 14

COMFORT IN ROUTINE

One would think that adolescents would rebel against a stringently imposed routine and schedule. Not so at Gross Breesen. The world of Jewish teenagers in Germany resembled concentric circles that spiraled inward. The outer circle was one of chaos and uncertainty. Nazi intrusion into every aspect of the Jews' lives could be counted on, but what form and when it would strike could not be predicted. Bondy knew this, and he so structured Gross Breesen to alleviate the turmoil that swirled in the minds and hearts of his students. The youngsters knew what the schedule was every day, every week. It provided comfort in the security of knowing what was coming. The spinning circles of the students' lives rotated and squeezed inward. He wanted to control as many of those circles as possible. He understood that the final circle, the one that enveloped the individual, was the most important. If one felt secure and confident within it, he could withstand just about anything. That's why the predictable life at Gross Breesen could be counted on. It was supposed to be that way.

THE SCHEDULE

In the early months of 1936, scheduling of activities was determined by the needs of an immediate project that required completion. Everyone woke at 5:00 a.m. That's the farmer's way. If there is daylight, work can be accomplished. In the winter, sunrise occurred later, but that didn't matter. Early morning classes followed breakfast. Meals and rest hour always followed the clock. Classes in the late afternoon and more classes after dinner were always anticipated. Sabbath services and the lighting of the Sabbath candles always occurred on Friday evenings. On Saturday mornings, Bondy convened the entire student body for life talks. On Sundays, there was mandatory attendance at a concert. Lights out with no talking commenced at 9:00 p.m. Totally exhausted, the students did not chafe under the early hour of retiring. Students at Gross Breesen slept soundly.

The routine also followed the growing and farming seasons. First, there was the haying in early summer with its long hours of collecting and storing in the barns. Second was the grain harvest, putting up sheaves, loading the dry sheaves onto wagons, unloading the wagons in the barn and stacking the sheaves at top speed. Third, between the end of the grain harvest and the beginning of winter, rows of potatoes, sugar beets and turnips had to be unearthed and stored. Fourth, after the vegetables were dug up, stones and rocks had to be picked as the fields were prepared for the next planting season. Fifth, hotbed mats were woven. Sixth, the threshing of the grains—wheat, barley and oats—was completed. Seventh, ice was harvested from the ponds to refrigerate produce in warmer weather, and trees were cut for lumber and heating. The girls had their chores, but whenever possible, they joined the boys in the fields. For the students, the schedule was punctual. Life was secure and purposeful.[78]

Chapter 15

THE DROUGHT

Töpper bent down and picked up a sack of grain. He hoisted it onto his shoulder and climbed the ladder to the loft floor. Then it dawned on him. He had just picked up a 150-pound sack and balanced it on a ladder! Where did he get that strength? He was not big or naturally strong, but he did it. How did that happen? Almost every chore at Gross Breesen was done by hand. In the fields, potatoes and turnips were picked by hand, one at a time. In Töpper's words, that was "sheer torture." Fertilizing with lime was spread by just flicking the wrist, and even spreading the dried manure was done by hand. But this was in 1930s Germany, not the Middle Ages. There were machines that could do all the chores faster and easier. So why was everything done by hand? There was a reason: without really being aware, the students were in training. Every day, they gained physical strength; muscles now contoured their arms and legs. They became toughened to the weather, tolerating hot or cold, wind or rain.

But there was another reason. By working so much with their hands, they became attached to the land. They kneaded the soil as if it were dough to be baked by the sun. And that is exactly what happened in the first summer. The days stretched on without rain. The sun cooked the soil, and it hardened and cracked. It was depressing, and to the surprise of the students, they felt like they were being parched as well. The students began to grasp the drama of farming: after doing everything right, preparing the land and planting the seeds, the farmer is helpless before nature. Without rain, there is only slow growth or just withering devastation.

The weeks dragged on, and no rain. One evening, when Bondy was speaking to the group, a clap of thunder shook the castle. He stopped in mid-sentence. Everyone listened in absolute silence, in hopeful anticipation. Then another clap that was louder than the first. A storm was approaching. And then it happened. The heavens let loose with a torrent of rain. There was a spontaneous cheer, and the students ran outside, leaving Bondy standing alone and speechless. The students pranced on the soaked lawn and flopped down to squirm like worms in the wet grass, and as they rolled and slid, blades of grass stuck to their clothes. They took off their shoes and felt the wet, cool mud squish between their toes. There was laughter and joyful screaming. Everyone became waterlogged. They opened their mouths to catch the drops and scrubbed their hair as if in the shower. The rain continued.

The students returned to the manor house dripping. They toweled themselves off and went to their rooms to put on dry pajamas. Bondy never finished the lesson for the night, but the students learned something much more important. They realized that they had connected to the land, that they cared so deeply about the crops and that Gross Breesen was more than just a school. It was their home and their farm.[79]

Chapter 16

HEARTACHE AND
GROWING UP

Maturing never follows one straight road. The curves and hills are numerous, and for most, sure-footed steps forward are followed by slipping and falling backward. Growing up is never easy, especially when one lives in abnormal times.

Töpper could be very emotional. His hot temper sometimes got him into trouble, and the other students often lost patience with him. They thought he was too sentimental and not tough enough to be a farmer, especially if he was going to settle in a strange new place somewhere in a new world. This bothered him immensely. One episode startled him deeply.

A fawn had been hit by a mowing machine and was severely injured. One of the instructors brought the fawn to Töpper so he could nurse it back to health. He carried the fawn to his room and hand-fed it. He stroked the fawn's head as if it were a family pet. After lights-out, he sneaked to where the fawn lay and whispered words of encouragement. The next morning, when Töpper excitedly approached the fawn, he realized it had died during the night from internal injuries. His reaction was extreme. He cried vehemently and could not be consoled. His grief spiraled out of control. His roommates finally could not tolerate his behavior. After all, they reasoned, it was only a fawn, not a person. Töpper buried the fawn in the woods and finally caught hold of himself. He knew that he had really lost it. He was humiliated. He had lost face.

Töpper separated himself from his bunkmates. In the solitude and quiet, he heard Bondy's probing questions in his mind. He asked himself his own troubling questions, Bondy questions, as never before: Why was he so uncontrollably agitated? Why was the grief so deep? Was he mourning for something other than the death of a fawn? Perhaps for the first time, Töpper could honestly ask himself these questions. He was willing to struggle with his own truths. He looked deeper into himself, faced up to what he saw and sought a strength that was buried behind his emotional outbursts. That is where he wanted to dwell, behind and beyond being a boy. Töpper had begun his journey to becoming a man. Bondy's perpetual mantra of learning about one's own deepest feelings, one's self-awareness, got through to him. Now those questions were his own.[80]

Tragedy hacks away like a machete and lays waste to everything that is expected or assumed to be in a future. There is no way to protect oneself from the slicing blade of anguish, and when tragedy hits young people, the blow is devastating. When a young person dies, the timetable of the universe is thrown out of whack. This happened to Töpper and his roommates three times in the first two years at Gross Breesen. One friend drowned on a sunny Sunday afternoon outing. The boys had ridden their bikes to a favorite swimming place on the Oder River. They plunged into the water, but one never surfaced. A second broke his neck innocently doing a gymnastics flip in the manor house, and incomprehensibly, a third committed suicide off campus. The youthful sense of immortality was shattered into tears and remorse. Young people are not supposed to die.[81]

Chapter 17

TÖPPER, THE SPOKESMAN

The dormitory rooms accommodated ten to twelve students who molded into families or teams, each naming itself, often after the eldest student or an assistant teacher. Time was allotted for bunk activities, and during free time, the roommates hung out together, both on and off the farm. One activity that knitted the students together was the weekly Sunday morning room inspections by Bondy. Fear has a way of unifying people. It was during inspection that Bondy reverted to his military ways. In the eyes of the boys, he approached being deranged. In preparation, Töpper, along with his partner, Prinz, tidied their metal wardrobe. The underwear, handkerchiefs, shirts and so on were folded precisely and piled on the appropriate shelves. The socks were laid flat in piles of three. Everyone polished their shoes. When Bondy entered the room, the boys stood at attention with their hearts pounding. He scanned the room silently and then hunted for dust on the radiators, the windowsills and the bed supports. He checked the blankets to determine if they were taut enough and folded correctly at the corners. He then turned to the wardrobes. He fingered the piles of clean, folded clothes, and if he determined that the folded clothes were not precise enough or, heaven forbid, he uncovered dirty clothes hidden behind clean ones, he would violently sweep his hand and throw the clothes onto the clean floor. His voice shrieked with accusations. As he left the room, silently seething, the floor looked like a battlefield. No matter that this ritual happened every week, the students never got used to the trauma.

After one such inspection, the boys of his bunk decided that Töpper should go to Bondy and present their thoughts about the inspection routine and the fear and emotional storm that always erupted. They gave Töpper a list of complaints and talked about what would be an effective way to communicate their feelings. As Töpper approached Bondy's door, the green light was lit. He rang the doorbell and entered the room. Bondy was on the sofa covered with a blanket. It was his naptime. Töpper wondered if he had picked the worst possible time to present the students' concerns. He pulled over a chair and sat next to the sofa. Bondy's eyes remained shut. For some unexplained reason, Töpper was not trembling. His voice was calm as he explained that he came as a delegate. He emphasized how emotionally draining the inspections were and wondered what impression was made on those newly arrived students. There was a long silence. Bondy did not open his eyes. Then he responded, "Thank you, Töpper, for speaking to me so openly. I will think about it." Töpper thanked Dr. Bondy and quietly left the room. He returned to his room where his friends sat stiffly as they listened in wide-eyed admiration. Töpper's mission proved successful. Bondy continued his inspections, but he toned them down. Töpper wondered if Bondy realized how difficult it was to bring up the subject and talk so truthfully. Obviously, he did.[82]

This was not the only instance when Töpper spoke up. Another time, he was the harbinger of some comic relief. It is easy to understand that adolescent boys and girls living together and working together had sexual urges and thoughts. Everyone knew, however, that if there was a sex-related "incident," the community's trust would be broken and the reputation and existence of Gross Breesen would be jeopardized. There was, however, an incident, but it was only a verbal one. One of the boys approached a girl, and in his exaggerated teenage fantasy, he asked her if she would go to bed with him. The girl refused, but she panicked and went to Bondy.

Late in the afternoon, Bondy called a meeting for the boys and another for the girls that would be run by Frau Scheier. Töpper had just come in from the field and was dirty and tired. Before he could clean up, he joined the others who were already sitting expectantly in the meeting room. All was deathly quiet. Bondy stood at the lectern and just glared at the boys in prolonged silence. This always meant that trouble was brewing. Finally, he slowly and gravely reported what had happened. The boy who made the "lewd" suggestion was immediately expelled and sent home. Bondy was incensed. He had stated before that any and all sexual contacts must wait until marriage. For the boys, ages fifteen to seventeen, marriage was so far in the distant future that they could not even imagine it. But Bondy did make sense. Sex could not be isolated from one's total behavior. It was part of a person's attitude. He explained, "What does matter is whether a person wants to live in accordance with moral principles and to what extent he makes an effort to put them into effect. We cannot be decent in one area of life and not in another one."[83] For the boys, sex was a very intriguing topic, and some were secretly amused observing Bondy being so self-conscious, but no one even shifted uncomfortably in his chair.

Whatever possessed Töpper, neither he nor anyone else could begin to understand. He raised his hand, and after being acknowledged by Bondy, he stood up to speak. He began by saying that because no girls were present, he felt comfortable with what he wanted to say. He stated the obvious: every boy, once or twice a month, worked with the girls in the laundry. Then he confessed his concern. "It's uncomfortable to have to handle male underwear that is soiled. Especially in front of girls. They have to do it all the time. We have plenty of toilet paper, so use it better." He sat down. There was not a giggle. Not even a smile. Everyone was absolutely astonished that Töpper would say this. There was resounding silence. Then Bondy spoke. "Töpper is absolutely right. Please make better efforts in this matter." He then signaled the end of the meeting, and all filed out quietly. Bondy's response was as bizarre as Töpper's observation. He could have erupted with venomous castigations at Töpper and the boys, but he didn't. Töpper, whether consciously or not, had sliced through the dreadful heaviness of the meeting and disarmed Herr Professor. One can only imagine the laughter that exploded in the dorm rooms once the doors were shut.[84]

Chapter 18

A RAY OF HOPE, 1938

Life at Gross Breesen resembled the purposeful buzzing of a human beehive. The students were becoming more skillful farmers, and the farm was largely self-sustaining. There was only one thing missing: positive news of when and where the students would emigrate from Germany. Most of the students had been in training for two years, and still there was no promise of relocating Gross Breeseners to a new country. When there was talk of a potential new settlement, spirits soared, but when the negotiations evaporated, spirits plummeted. The students felt like yo-yos. Plans to settle in Brazil and Argentina fell through, sometimes because of unrealizable preconditions of governments, such as conversion to Christianity. The pattern became starkly defined. Countries throughout the world slammed their doors to immigrants and refugees even as Germany's persecution increased. Even Bondy was growing anxious. He wrote in the *CV Newspaper*: "A serious impediment to our work arose by the fact that the prospects for a community settlement have gradually diminished during the last year. One project after another proved to be unachievable."[85]

Finally, there was a ray of hope. It appeared from New York City in early winter 1938. A member of the original governing body of the German Jewish community that created Gross Breesen,

Friedrich Borchardt, was working in the United States for the Joint Distribution Committee, an organization that raised money to support desperate Jews in Europe and also help them immigrate to safe havens throughout the world. One night, as he was reviewing his files, Borchardt came across a letter with the heading "Thalhimer Department Store." He paused for a moment and flipped through his mental database. Like a search on a computer, Thalhimer's name flashed: department store owner in Richmond, Virginia; Jewish; national chairman for the Resettlement of German Jewish Refugees in America. Borchardt's curiosity was piqued. In the letter, William B. Thalhimer proposed that he purchase a farm for German Jewish refugees who would learn farming and then become self-supporting. Borchardt jumped out of his chair, and even though he was dead tired, his eyes snapped wide open. Was there hope? Could this Thalhimer rescue the students of Gross Breesen?

Borchardt inquired about Thalhimer and immediately contacted him to make sure that he was serious about his proposal. After a telephone conversation, he was reassured; he had to take a risk, a leap of faith. He telegrammed Bondy to arrange for a meeting between the two men set for February. No one at Gross Breesen knew about this. There was no need to raise expectations again. As Bondy flew to England and boarded the ship to New York where he and Thalhimer would meet, he knew that the world was slamming closed all gates of entry. So much rode on Thalhimer.

The two men extended their hands in welcome. Their eyes met, and for a brief moment, each looked into the soul of the other. Then smiles erupted. Each knew the other immediately. Without words spoken, the pain that German Jews were feeling was held in the palms of their handshake. Their personalities meshed. They both were no-nonsense men urgently committed to rescuing Jewish students from Germany and, particularly, those at Gross Breesen. As they departed, their handshake was firm and their smiles encouraged. Bondy was certain about Thalhimer. He left New York with renewed hope

In April, Bondy received the telegram that he was waiting for. Thalhimer had found a farm, but before he would purchase it, he needed Bondy to evaluate it and give his approval. He traveled to

The Civil War–era main house at Hyde Farmlands, Burkeville, Virginia, 1939. *Courtesy of the Eva Loew collection.*

Virginia, inspected the farm and gave Thalhimer his enthusiastic and thankful blessing. It was a large 1,500-acre working farm in rural Burkeville, Virginia, several hours south of Thalhimer's home in Richmond. There was a large manor house that would house students and staff, much as the castle did. It needed to be renovated, but it would be perfect.

Now Bondy could tell the students there was a "Virginia Plan." There was much excitement, but U.S. immigration visas had to be procured—not an easy matter. Bondy did not want to dampen enthusiasm, but he cautioned the students that there were still many hurdles that had to be crossed.

In April 1938, the clock was ticking for Jews living in Germany; time was running out. Immediately, Bondy traveled to the U.S. consulate in Berlin to meet with Consul General Raymond Geist. As he rode the train, he was nervous. Would he be able to describe the Gross Breesen experience adequately, convince Geist that the students were worthy and begin to arrange for applying for visas for the students? He knew that there were nearly insurmountable roadblocks in the immigration process, but at least this was a start. There was so much riding on this first encounter. As Bondy approached the consulate, his mind took a snapshot of the scene. In front of him was a helmeted German soldier standing guard, with a rifle at his side. He stood within a fenced booth that elevated him above the street. The soldier constantly scanned the area, his head turning side to side as if he were the beacon in a lighthouse. Questions raced through Bondy's mind as he eyed the stone building: How would the meeting go? Was there any possibility to acquire visas? Would the consul general be receptive and sympathetic? Could the two communicate effectively in German or in his own halting English? Bondy had been briefed about Raymond Geist. He was a man very well known by the Jewish community, though he, himself, was not Jewish. He was a very influential diplomat, and he knew and socialized with the top Nazi officials in order to infiltrate the Nazi bureaucracy to gain valuable information for the U.S. State Department. Bondy had sent a pamphlet about Gross Breesen to Geist before the meeting. In it, Bondy explained the curriculum, but it was the intangible values, the "Gross Breesen Spirit," that he wanted to convey. In his mind, it was the values, the hard work and the long hours the students endured that made them worthy candidates for immigration to America. The two conversed in German. Geist listened intently and was impressed with Gross Breesen and Bondy's limitless commitment to the welfare of his students. In return, Bondy sensed Geist's desire to help. He learned later that the next day, the consul translated the Gross Breesen informational pamphlet from German into English and sent it to the State Department in Washington, D.C. Bondy left the meeting feeling less anxious, though he wondered what would happen next. Would the students and staff receive visas, and how soon could they emigrate and land on America's shores to begin work on Thalhimer's farm?

On the train ride back to Gross Breesen, Bondy began to compile a list of twenty-five students he thought would be the best candidates for the Virginia Plan. These students had to be the most promising because the Virginia Plan could not fail. It had to become a model community for other future successes. Bondy felt an enormous responsibility to Thalhimer and to the students who would immigrate.

Even though Eva had not yet been at Gross Breesen a full year, Bondy placed her on the Virginia list. He was sure that she would be a strong member of the new community. Töpper was also included in the twenty-five. Obviously, Bondy thought that he had boundless potential. When the names were posted, some of the girls who had been at Gross Breesen much longer than Eva were upset. They questioned why she was selected before them, but that calmed down very quickly.[86]

The farm that Thalhimer had purchased in April was magnificent. It had an impressive pedigree. It dated back to the 1750s as a land grant by the king of England. It survived the Revolutionary War and the Civil War, with its sixty slaves, and now it hopefully would become a haven for German Jewish refugees. Its new name was Hyde Farmlands, in honor of the old name, Hyde Park Farm. Now Thalhimer needed the students from Gross Breesen to refurbish it and make it productive again. The first growing season in central Virginia had already begun, so the sooner the students could arrive and begin farming, the better.

In June, the first Gross Breesener, Ernst Loewensberg, an assistant to Bondy, arrived at Hyde Farmlands. He had already immigrated to the United States through the urging and help of family members. His letters, written under the light of a kerosene lamp and sent to Gross Breesen, captured his excited observations: "I can only tell you that it is exceptionally suitable for our purpose. Twenty-two rooms are available to us. Some bigger, some smaller. They are only waiting for a painter, who can beautify them…On the first floor is a splendid balcony and I can imagine that we will place our musicians there, while we sit below in the grass and listen to them."[87]

He was expansive in his reporting. There were stables, "called barns in English," and two new muscular workhorses, a breed rare in the South that Thalhimer had purchased with special pride. He wrote about the farm's forest that "contains a source of great wealth in good timber and fertile arable land…There is not going to be a shortage of forest work."[88]

In his description, Ernst noted that the living conditions were primitive compared to Gross Breesen: no running water in the manor house, no showers and only outhouses. Buckets drawn from the well supplied all the water needed for cooking, washing and watering the animals. His keen eye studied how the locals farmed, and he was thrilled that they were so friendly and willing to share their knowledge of local farming. They were curious about his life back in Germany, as they always asked questions and wanted to see photographs of Gross Breesen. Ernst reveled in the exciting details of his new life at Hyde Farmlands, and he yearned for the time when more students would join him at their new Virginia home. He ended his letters by reminding the anxious readers: "When we are all here, then on such days we will put the farm in order. In accordance with the proven model [Gross Breesen]. We have had plenty of practice in that. And everyone knows what work he has then to do." With happy anticipation, he concluded one of his letters: "When I write the next report, Haka [another Gross Breesener] will be here!"[89] Ernst was hopeful that his good news would excite and encourage those who had been selected to immigrate to America. Indeed, he stoked the fire of yearning in those who could only hope. How frustrated they were because they had already trained for two years, and they were still stuck in Germany.

The students asked what Mr. Thalhimer was like. Bondy was gratified to relate that Thalhimer was an unusual man of goodwill who shared the same values as he held dear. He had been working with the relocation of German Jewish immigrants ever since his trip to Germany in 1930, when he encountered a Brown Shirt rally and witnessed how the Nazis were treating Jews. Now, eight years later, he was the national chairman of the Refugee Resettlement Committee of the National Coordinating Committee, the umbrella organization for Jewish immigration to the United States. A Jew himself, people looked to him for advice as they came from all over the country. Thalhimer was as excited by the prospects of having Gross Breesen students come to Virginia as Bondy was.

Eva listened to Ernst's letters intently. Something special about Ernst caught her attention. She was thrilled by his spirit of adventure and confidence. She could picture him driving the powerful workhorses that pulled the plow churning the soil. She imagined his glistening, muscular arms grasping the wooden handles of the plow. She could hear the leather reins snapping on the backs of the horses and the metal bridle clanging as he shouted commands to the team. She could smell the fresh soil

Ernst Loewensberg plows the field with his prized workhorses at Hyde Farmlands. *Courtesy of the Eva Loew collection.*

upturned into farrows packed solidly and shining metal-like from the compression of the plow. She could see the slow movement of the plowed soil folding onto itself like breaking waves progressing down a beach. She wanted to work with this Ernst Loewensberg. She wanted to settle at Hyde Farmlands.

Chapter 19

THE POSTCARD
TO TÖPPER

Work activities at Gross Breesen became more efficient and productive as the year progressed. The community melded with a sense of high purpose and anticipation that emigration would come soon. Töpper was confident and energetic, until he came down with a persistent skin infection on his chest in mid-September. Ilse Lehmann, the doctor at Gross Breesen, who had been stripped of her hospital affiliation because she was Jewish, urged Töpper to go to the Breslau Jewish Hospital for treatment. Once there, he thought the hospital was just not clean or efficient enough, and after several phone calls home, he received permission to return to Berlin for treatment. In typical Töpper fashion, without going through the customary sign-out formalities, he snuck out of the hospital at night, "threw his little bag over the wall, climbed over, and took the next train to Berlin."[90]

By mid-October, the infection was cured, and he could not wait to see his friends and get back into the routine of work and study. He was relieved to leave Nazified Berlin. His return to Gross Breesen was met with a joyful reception, but his exuberance was short-lived because of a postcard he received from his father:

FROM NAZI GERMANY TO THALHIMER'S FARM

19 October 1937
My dear Töpper, I am writing to you at this unusual time for
a reason. I must speak to you, and ask you to come to Berlin on
Saturday with a weekend ticket. Monday noon you'll go back to
Breesen. Don't ask any questions…we will talk about it when
you're here…a big kiss, Papa.[91]

Töpper was mystified, especially since he had just been home.
When he returned to Berlin, he found that his father had flown to
Amsterdam to make arrangements for the family to go to England
and then immigrate to somewhere as yet determined. Töpper's jaw
dropped. He had no idea that the family was fleeing Germany, and
on top of that, he had no intentions of going with them. His place
was at Gross Breesen, and he fully anticipated immigrating with his
friends as a group to a farm colony somewhere else. His mother left
him alone in the house for a few hours. He related years later, "My
head was spinning. The thought of having to leave Gross Breesen
and my friends so suddenly, to break off my training, maybe never to
settle overseas with my friends, was more than I could handle at that
moment."[92] In the quiet of the apartment, he made up his mind.
He would disobey his parents, stand up for what he wanted and
return to Gross Breesen. He selected a few books from the family
library and hurriedly made his way to the railroad station, heading
for Breslau and then to Gellendorf.

From the railroad station, Töpper lugged his heavy suitcase to
the Schloss. Bondy met him at the door and invited him to his room
to talk over the situation. Afterward, Töpper went to his room,
shoved his suitcase under his bed and went to Scheier to get his
work assignment for the following day. He was determined to stay,
and he thought he would.

But he couldn't stay. Bondy went to Berlin to confer with the
organization that sponsored Gross Breesen and also to discuss the
matter with Töpper's father. The decision was final. Töpper had
to leave with his family. If he didn't, the Nazi authorities could
arrest him and use him as a hostage to force his family to return to
Germany and return the money they intended to smuggle out of
the country, which was against the national currency regulations. In

addition, the Nazis could close down Gross Breesen in retaliation for his father's illegal actions. Töpper had just a few days to prepare himself for his departure from Gross Breesen. He was distraught, but he promised Bondy that he would not reveal all the facts of why he was leaving. The Gestapo should not find out. On the day before he was to depart, there was a brief farewell by Bondy. Then the string quartet played Tchaikovsky's "Italian Capriccio," which was Töpper's favorite piece. He was accompanied by Leus, his girlfriend, to the railroad station. They hugged and kissed and cried.

Töpper looked out into the dark night from the train window. He believed his life and dreams were being crushed. He could not believe that the year and a half of joy at Gross Breesen was over. He could not hold back the tears. He was suffering. There were so many questions, but the most important one was written in bold black print in his mind: **Would he be able to emigrate with his Gross Breesen friends when the time came?** Bondy assured him that "someplace, sometime in the future" he would, but it seemed so hard to believe.[93] Where would he get the courage to go on without Gross Breesen?

Töpper left Gross Breesen in October 1937. Though Eva hardly knew him, she listened to many Töpper stories. They did not know it at the time, but their lives would be intertwined in the near future and for the rest of their lives.

Chapter 20

A TELEPHONE CALL TO EVA

One could safely say that Eva "ate up" everything about Gross Breesen: the heavy work, the study load and the comradery. She adopted the Gross Breesen motto, "K.S." ("keep smiling"), and added it to her own time-tested personal motto: "This too shall pass."[94] She threw herself into every activity and absorbed the values and goals of Bondy. She simply loved Gross Breesen.

So it was a shock when she received a telephone call from her mother. The message was starkly blunt: "Pack up everything, and as fast as you can, come home." There was no further explanation.[95] The Jacobsohns had made a decision now that all Jewish physicians had lost their licenses to practice medicine. In addition, German friends, some Nazi Party members, secretly warned them that life for Jews was deteriorating rapidly, so they needed to flee Germany at once. Now it was time to act.

That August night, Eva went for a walk out in the fields with a few of her friends. She would never forget the sweet smell of the harvested wheat—the very wheat she had planted. Then she walked to the railroad tracks that would take her to Breslau the next day. The open view of the night sky at the tracks was panoramic. She gazed silently. She always half-joked that she talked with the constellations and inhaled their cosmic breath.

Just as she nuzzled her face into a sunflower, so she had face-to-face encounters with the Big Dipper.

The girls reminisced about the time when they stood on the tracks and a thunderstorm approached from three sides. The fast-moving storm provided a gray background to the sun-painted, golden wheat fields, and the turbulent winds drove the wheat into wide, waving swathes. Lightning and thunder crashed from far off, and the warm wind bathed them.[96]

The next day, Eva was driven to the Gellendorf railroad station. Gross Breesen was sad to say goodbye. She was a spark plug, an energy source that motivated others. She graced the grand hall of the Schloss when she played the grand piano. She was disheartened to leave her new friends and everything about Gross Breesen, but she was fortified with the knowledge that she was on the Virginia Plan list. She knew something very important was about to take place. Otherwise, her mother would not have called her home so suddenly, though she did not really know what to expect. She arrived home late in the afternoon.

Chapter 21

EVA'S ESCAPE

Anti-Semitism in Germany blatantly increased. Emigrating was becoming more difficult, and taking one's possessions and money out of the country was nearly impossible, but the Jacobsohn family had help. During World War I, Dr. Jacobsohn made a promise to a dying patient that he would look after the soldier's wife and two sons. He kept his word, and in the years that followed the war, he became a surrogate father to those two sons. When Hitler came to power, Eva's father advised the eldest son to accept a commission as a SS officer. In the late summer of 1938, that officer appeared at the Jacobsohns' door under the cover of night. He was nervous. His words were straight to the point: "Get out of Germany, now." He had risked much to convey that warning. If he were seen aiding Jews, he certainly would have lost his commission, and perhaps worse. But he did risk it all. His debt of gratitude to Dr. Jacobsohn for taking care of his family transcended military duty and Nazi Party affiliation. To that officer, the Jacobsohns were not just Jews; they were family.[97]

As the situation for Jews worsened, the Jacobsohns housed desperate relatives and friends who had lost their homes and incomes. Mrs. Jacobsohn was the family decision-maker. She was the one who sensed the gravity of the situation early on and now determined it was time to leave Germany as soon as possible. The visit from the SS officer finally convinced her husband, though he was still hesitant. If it were not for Eva's mother, the family would never have left, and they probably would not have survived the Holocaust death camps of the 1940s. She responded to the deteriorating chaos with resolve. She procured the exit visas for Eva and her sister Hannah and packed the items they should take with them. She supervised the packing up of the household items in large wooden crates that she wanted to take to the United States. Exit visas were almost impossible to obtain as tens of thousands of Jews tried to leave Germany all at once, but a patient of Dr. Jacobsohn's worked in the visa office and expedited the necessary paperwork to provide exit visas for the family members. He, too, had to function secretly beyond the sight of the Nazis.

On August 22, 1938, Eva and Hannah walked out the front door of their home and locked the door. Their parents had left for Cuba several days before. They each carried a suitcase. Eva's was heavy because she had stuffed it with what she loved most: her books. They walked down their tree-lined sidewalk as if nothing peculiar was happening, as if the two were leaving on an ordinary vacation or a visit. Not even stopping, they turned to glance back at their home for the last time before they turned the corner.

From Berlin, the two sisters flew to Zurich, Switzerland. They could not travel through France because it would have taken too much time to obtain transit permits. They stayed with family friends for a few weeks and then flew directly to England. There, they reunited with Eva's elder sister, Ruth, and her younger brother, Heine, in London. In England, everyone carried a gas mask because the population expected war to break out at any moment.

Eva and Hannah boarded the Holland-American ocean liner the *Statendam* on October 1 and set sail for America. Her parents had telegrammed the girls earlier from Cuba that they should rejoin them there, for that is where they were granted entry. For the present, Ruth and Heine were to remain in England.

The ship slowly turned from the mainland and ventured out to sea. On the deck, the passengers gazed back at the landmass as its details of buildings, moored ships and coastline contours faded into a phantom cloud of mist. The ship rocked, as if to remind the passengers that their familiar human home on solid ground no longer existed. They were now in an alien world that had no resemblance to the life that anchored them before. This was a universal response, but for Eva, the reality had particular meaning. She was once again in exile, but not like before when she was in England and could return home. Now there was no home to return to. As she held on to the rail, peering off into the distance, she reached for her pocketbook that was slung across her shoulder. She grasped her passport and looked at it for a long time. It was her ticket to freedom. The Nazis had amended it. She focused on the red "J" for *Juden*, Jew, and the name given to all Jewish women, "Sara." She muttered an anguished question that no one could hear except herself: "What on earth have we all done, that now things are so hard instead of living in peace?" She talked to herself: "You can't change things when circumstances are stronger than what you can do. You can't put your head through a wall because the wall keeps standing there, and all you do is get a bloody head. In Breesen, we used to say K.S. Keep smiling and make the best of it."[98] She acknowledged the anger that came over her. What did the Nazis know about her? All they saw was that she was a Jew, not even a German anymore. But she now possessed a plan: the Virginia Plan. She vowed not to look backward.

On the first day out to sea, off in the distance, "the sky ahead was a drab lilac color, but overhead the sun was still shining. The water had a very dark blue green color, and every place the whitecaps were blinking…The [wind] roared so much throughout the masts that you really couldn't hear your own words."[99] It was a threatening sign when the crew bolted down the heavy iron covers of the portholes. Then the storm hit. The waves rose with each new wind gust. Deck chairs slid from one side to the other. One woman's raincoat was ripped right off her from the wind. Sea spray exploded every time the bow cut through a rolling wave. The passengers scurried to their rooms. At night, the hall that was scheduled to host the gala departure party was almost vacant. Waiters stood around with nothing to do, but Eva could eat even as others were deathly seasick.

Eva's Nazi-issued passport. Between August and October 1938, all legal documents were stamped "J" for Jew, "Sara" for all Jewish females and "Israel" for all Jewish men. *Courtesy of the Eva Loew collection.*

The storm worsened. At one point, the ship cut its engines and tossed helplessly. Its forward motion had stopped altogether. Water had flooded the engine room, and all hands were ordered to man the pumps. The ship dropped into the deep caverns between the wave crests, so low that one lost sight of the horizon. It was totally unnerving to look to the side of the ship and see nothing but a wall of ocean. Some of the waves reached gigantic heights taller than houses. This had all the earmarks of a hurricane. The passengers were sick and frightened, but Eva found the entire experience thrilling, though scary. In her diary, she wrote, "With the storm, you realized that nature does not let itself be controlled by man. Such a great force makes people completely helpless."[100] This was a tumultuous beginning to her new life.

The voyage that began with such ferocity ended in the quiet calm that follows a storm. As the sun broke through the clouds, the passengers timidly appeared on deck. Most had never met the other passengers because they had stayed in their rooms throughout the storm. At night, Eva stood at the rail and studied the night sky. "The moon was out…pieces of clouds shot by the moon…the strange coloring of the ocean was actually unbelievable."[101] As the ship entered New York Harbor, Eva marveled at how everything looked "exactly the way one saw it in the movies or the way it was written about in books. The Statue of Liberty really looked small next to the skyscrapers."[102] As the passengers disembarked, the two sisters became stuck in bureaucratic quicksand. For seven hours they tried to clarify to the authorities that they possessed transit visas, good for only four days staying in the United States, before they traveled to Cuba. Eva's aunt waited for the girls on the pier; they were the last to leave the ship. They were exhausted but relieved that the longest part of the journey was over. In a few days, they would board a banana freighter, the SS *Mexico*, which carried only sixty passengers, and travel south to reunite with their parents in Cuba.

The night they left New York Harbor, a thick fog bank enveloped the boat. Every two minutes, the ship's foghorn blared. Falling asleep was impossible. Nevertheless, Eva was falling in love with sailing. The first day out, the ocean was a mirror, and it was hot. As the day proceeded, rain clouds appeared on the horizon. The sun reflected off the raindrops and formed the most beautiful rainbow that Eva had ever seen. The sunset was extravagant with deep reds, yellows and then dark green and finally night blue. As the sunset lingered in the west, Eva relaxed in a deck chair outside her cabin. "The wind started up and light and dark clouds with strange configurations went by so that [she] felt like a witness to a giant theatre production."[103] To Eva's surprise, the night air did not cool down. Every mile traveled south brought the boat closer to the heat of Cuba.

In just a matter of weeks, Eva had traveled through a world of contrasts. She felt like she was on a carousel, and as her imaginary, galloping horse circled around, she scanned the painted scenes of distant and exotic lands. Indeed, she was on a merry-go-round: first Germany and then to Switzerland. Then in the air to England and an ocean journey to New York. Next, the slow sailing into a completely different climate heading south to Cuba. All this within just two weeks.

The banana boat sighted the island of Cuba. At first, it was just a dot floating on the horizon that bobbed up and down, but as the boat approached the island, it loomed larger and the ocean seemed to shrink. Eva knew that she would be entering a new world of smells, colors, trees and flowers, music and people who spoke a language she did not understand. Her parents met the boat with smiles of relief. Their daughters had made the trip safely, and now they were together again, even though they were in a strange new land.

CUBA

Instead of feeling insecure and strange, Eva was invigorated by every new experience that Cuba offered. Dr. and Mrs. Jacobsohn had friends in Cuba who embraced them warmly and introduced the family to the Cuban way of life. On the first trip out to their farm, the three-hour train ride afforded Eva a view of the countryside. She saw sugar cane fields for the first time, and she noticed that the soil was rust-colored. The train passed through villages, orange and lemon groves and beautifully tailored gardens managed by Chinese farmers. There were pastures and fields where horses and cows were grazing. "Far away, [one] could see the mountain range and the sky was lit up in unbelievable colors as the sun was just going down. It was unbelievably beautiful, this picture of big royal palm trees silhouetted against the fiery evening sky."[104] After the train ride, the guests climbed onto oxen-drawn wooden carts with two huge wooden wheels. The jarring ride over pot-holed dirt roads took an hour and a half. The friends' single-story farmhouse was located at the edge of a small village. After the guests settled in and ate supper, Eva went outside before going to bed. As she wrote in her diary:

> *There was really a very eerie quiet and stillness about the land. It was very dark, so one could see all the stars which certainly [could not] be seen in the city. The stars here seem to have a much stranger and brighter glow than in Europe, and that's how you know that you are really completely somewhere else. The moon doesn't stand in the sky, but is lying down which at first is a very strange sight. Especially clearly we could see the Milky Way and then we went to bed.*[105]

Her sleep ended early in the morning when roosters crowed. After breakfast, Eva observed cowboys on horseback bringing the cows and their calves to a barn. She watched with fascination as the calves began to suck the mothers' teats, but then they were pulled away and the cowboys milked the cows for the milk that was needed for the day. Eva could not contain herself and jumped in to milk a cow. The men watched in astonishment, for here was a "city girl" who knew exactly how to manage the cow and milk it efficiently. After her show of skill and familiarity, the men clapped in appreciation.

One new experience followed another. Eva rode a horse for the first time and loved it. She was a natural as she learned to trot and gallop. As she rode past small farms, she realized how poor the people were. They had nothing, not even shoes for the children, but she mused to herself, "So much missing for them, and yet they are content."[106] Eva's world was expanding. She came from a cosmopolitan life in Berlin and London to the castle farm of Gross

Breesen and now to the primitive countryside of a third world country. Everything interested her. She rose early to view the tropical sunrise and then investigate the big pumping stations for irrigation and study the giant diesel motor that ran the pumps. She reveled in the slower pace of the life and the music, and she marveled at the natural dexterity of the natives dancing the rumba. She walked into a field and broke off a piece of sugar cane, peeled off the hard skin and sucked the sweet marrow. She asked questions about growing sugar cane and was impressed that after each harvest, the fields were burned and the soil was turned under and allowed to sit for several years before another crop was planted. She loved the Cuban landscape, especially the open fields, the caves and the beaches with the seashells and multicolored jellyfish. She was fascinated by the agave plant from which rope was made. The family visited Catholic churches and marveled at the pictures and sculptures of the saints. One young priest impressed Eva: "When he was talking about holy things, his face was uplifted unbelievably beautifully."[107]

In late January 1939, Eva's mother received her U.S. visa and immediately traveled to Miami to go through immigration. This

Eva discovered her love of horses during her short stay in Cuba. *Courtesy of the Eva Loew collection.*

meant that Eva and her sister were automatically granted visas and they could immigrate to America. "It is a wonderful feeling to know that the period of waiting is now at an end. And I can hardly wait for the time when we finally leave."[108] The plan was that Eva's mother would take her two daughters to Miami; Hannah would then travel to Texas to a family that would take her in, and Eva would go to New York to collect her baggage and then travel to Hyde Farmlands in Burkeville, Virginia. Dr. Jacobsohn could not enter the United States because he technically was of Polish nationality and had to wait for a Polish visa. He was eventually aided in his application by a Quaker organization in the United States and by a supporting letter sent to the State Department by the famous Albert Einstein, a friend of Jacobsohn.

Chapter 22

"ROOT HOLDS" AT HYDE FARMLANDS

Eva left her sister and mother in Miami and traveled to New York to retrieve her luggage. All she could think about was getting to Hyde Farmlands as soon as possible. From New York, she bussed to Burkeville and was picked up by the red farm truck, driven by Haka. He and Ernst were the first Breeseners to live on the farm, and now that Eva joined them, he was overjoyed. As they drove up the long, gravel driveway, Eva thought the farm was exactly as she had imagined it. She easily understood what Thalhimer and his cousin Morton saw in the place when they first evaluated it. She marveled at its size and buildings, and she also saw the potential to house a sizable Gross Breesen contingent. Through the back door, she entered the long, sun-filled kitchen. Immediately after she walked through a house tour given by Ernst, she changed from her traveling clothes of dress, heels and stockings. How good it felt to put on broken-in denim overalls and an everyday blouse with sleeves rolled up, and before she pulled up her soft, smooth, leather work boots, she hugged them and sniffed them as if they were a pet dog. Those leather boots, with their hard protective toes, spoke volumes. They had followed her from Gross Breesen to Cuba and now to Virginia. Now she felt like the authentic Eva.

After she hung up her clothes and arranged a small writing desk with a few books, notepaper, an ink bottle and her fountain pen, she walked outside to be alone for a while and explore the grounds. She politely refused a tour by the residents and set out to wander before sunset. She walked out the front door under the open porch that extended from the second floor. She studied everything, trying to take it all in. The red brick porch floor was a bit slippery because of a glaze of moss. She walked away from the house, far enough that when she turned and looked back, the perspective would be a wide one. Her first impression was dramatic and romantic. With affluent, substantive pillars and a sweeping porch, the white mansion stood tall and proud of its southern heritage. The long, dark windows invited her imagination to envision 1800s social events with women in flowing gowns and men in top hats, the scenes she had read in books and viewed in the movies. The level front lawn with its huge trees had a hint of spring green. The white exterior of the grand plantation house resembled a giant albino whale gracefully rolling out of an ocean of sea-lawn. Eva's literary imagination flew into full flight. The early spring air smelled sweet and moist as it cooled

Eva finally arrived at the Burkeville, Virginia bus station. *Courtesy of the Eva Loew collection.*

rapidly in the late afternoon. The buds on the trees were fully pregnant, straining to contain their own bursting into blossom. The readiness for another growth season was palpable. The ground was soft but not muddy. March in Virginia advances toward summer far ahead of its equivalent in Germany.

She walked around the side of the house to study the numerous farm structures in the back acres. There were barns, sheds and an old building that once housed a kitchen and slaves. Her eyes focused on a rundown cemetery that she planned to investigate later. Off in the distance, she saw a rough-hewn, smallish barn and what looked like a larger dairy barn. She headed out to investigate, walking the red dirt road that led west of the main house. The windowless structure was empty, but it had an odor that was unfamiliar to her. There was a wood-burning stove and rows of thin, stick rafters stretched overhead like a spider web. She wondered what these barns were used for. Across the road from the shed was a dairy barn. Her head swirled with the memories of the dairy barn at Gross Breesen. There was so much more to explore, but the sun was weakening, and she realized it

Eva was curious about the history found in the Hyde Farmlands cemetery. *Courtesy of Robert Gillette.*

Eva loved her "own" dairy barn at Hyde Farmlands. *Courtesy of the Eva Loew collection.*

would be rude not to pay attention to her fellow settlers who were anxious to talk with her.

Within just an hour, she felt at home. That night, after she wrote in her diary, she slept soundly. In the morning, she awoke to the crowing of a rooster. She could not stop grinning. She just lay in bed listening to the farm world wake up. A cow mooed, birds sang, donkeys brayed and Eva giggled. By early summer, there were seven Gross Breesen farmers—four men and three women—at Hyde Farmlands. The group worked seamlessly to prepare the farm and the living quarters for the other students who were expected to arrive at any moment, or so they thought. The farm manager, U.K. Franken, and his family lived in a wing of the main house. Franken had been hired by Thalhimer to ensure that the labor and the objectives for renovation were reasonable and on target. Before the women joined the workforce, Franken was quoted in the local *Crewe Chronicle*: "[I am] very optimistic over the spirit of cooperation that the young German boys are showing towards the program of the farm work outlined for the year 1939. These youngsters are fast becoming oriented, and in the short space of time that they have been located here, they have become 'good neighbors.'"[109]

At Hyde Farmlands, Eva gave "her" calves special attention. Here she teaches a calf to eat from a pail. *Courtesy of the Eva Loew collection.*

The transplanted Breeseners lived harmoniously, and each had specific responsibilities: Trudi looked after the pigs; Eva specialized in running the dairy; Ernst and Manfred managed the horse teams and plowing; Haka drove the truck and also focused on administrative concerns; Howard operated the tractor; and Lu was an all-around contributor. Lu's mother, "Mrs. A.," an American who lived in Germany before returning home, helped with the cooking, kept the young people in line and taught them the "American way" with everything. In addition to their specific responsibilities, everyone worked on whatever project needed attention at that moment. When it was time to seed, they all seeded; when it was time to harvest, they all picked and stored. They loved their work as they saw steady progress. Thalhimer came to visit, and he was impressed with the students' spirit and extensive accomplishments. He wrote to Bondy, "I like them all and would take every one of them into my family."[110]

Even though there was no running water or electricity in the main house, unlike Gross Breesen, all the chores were done without great difficulty. Cooking on the large wood stove, which also heated water, at first was a challenge because the cooking temperature fluctuated. But in no time, Eva learned the country way to gauge the oven's temperature by sticking her elbow into the oven and making a determination to extend or shorten cooking time. The water was hauled from the well located near the kitchen door, and the rusted chain that dropped into the well stained the workers' hands orange. Clothes were boiled clean in an enormous iron cauldron outside. Even the boys helped with the washing, as they also helped with kitchen cleanup in order to free the girls to attend to other chores. The cutting and splitting of cooking stove wood and fuel to fire the central steam heat furnace in the basement were crucial. The only skunky and sometimes scary part of this more primitive existence was the outhouses in the backyard. These "necessaries" were cold in the winter and "nasty" in the hot summer, and at night, when one was alone, they were downright scary. Because Eva had ample first aid training with her father, she served as the farm nurse who responded to the minor injuries of farm work.

Mrs. Franken was helpful and friendly, and her youngest boy, Scotty, became the mascot. The Piggs, tenant farmers who lived on the property, were also friendly, and they were instrumental in teaching the refugees how to farm tobacco. Eva learned that the odd smell she could not discern on her first day's exploration was that of tobacco curing.

Above: Eva (left) preparing a meal at Hyde Farmlands. Notice the water tank above the wood stove before electrification was installed in 1939. *Courtesy of the Eva Loew collection.*

Left: The boys shared household duties at Hyde Farmlands. Here, Ernst Loewensberg washes work clothes by boiling them. The cauldron still exists at Hyde Farmlands. *Courtesy of the Eva Loew collection.*

FROM NAZI GERMANY TO THALHIMER'S FARM

Eva could not have been happier. With the crossing of the Atlantic, she was now not only in a different place geographically but also in a new and exciting place in her own self. The constricting, German traditional role for women no longer held sway. Certainly, she still cooked and cleaned, did laundry and darned socks, but now she had greater responsibilities, jobs that "really mattered." She wrote, "So now, the whole cattle raising is in my hands. That sounds very arrogant, however, for it consists only of two cows, one heifer and one calf."[111] In addition, her previous gardening experience at home and at Gross Breesen exploded into a full-blown passion. She read everything she could get her hands on that related to dairying and truck farming. Soon, the two cows grew to six, so now, milking the cows twice a day and their care occupied huge chunks of her time. Her training at Gross Breesen paid off, and she wished that the ober could see her new dairy and how well she was managing. How proud she was that she could milk so efficiently that foam formed on top of the milk in the pail. This was always an indication of an expert dairy person. A friendly neighbor, Mr. Hamlin, adored Eva, and on her birthday, he presented her with her own heifer. She rigorously studied the mouth-watering bulletins published by the Virginia Cooperative Service, and her most cherished book became her bible, the *1938 Dairy Production Manual* published by Virginia Polytech Institute (known today as Virginia Tech University). When the extension agents came to visit the farm, Eva peppered them with questions. The agents marveled at her growing knowledge and insights. In fact, they were equally impressed with the work ethic and congeniality of all the refugees. They voiced their admiration many times by stating that they wished all young American farmers would be as committed and hardworking.

The year's study at St. Paul's Girls' School prepared Eva more than she could ever have imagined when she was going through such personal torment. Eva's spoken English was very good, so she became the go-to person whenever the group interacted with the outside world. She looked forward to traveling to the nearby towns and to Richmond to purchase seed and supplies for the farm. Seed and feed retailers were men-only establishments. If there were any women around, they would only be found away from the selling

Eva saved the original labels from the seed bags she purchased for the farm to establish a work-related archive. *Courtesy of the Eva Loew collection.*

floor in the office as secretaries. Not so for Eva. She walked onto the floor with authority and discussed the attributes of the various seeds with the Southern States salesmen, and she drove a tough bargain. Thalhimer paid for the seed, but Eva made sure that he was never overcharged. She knew what was needed on the farm and calculated the quantities exactly. It did not take long for the counter salesmen to look forward to Eva's visits. They joked with her in the only way they knew, farmer jokes and male oriented, but they were always impressed by her gentle toughness and probing questions. "Here comes Eva," they would call. "Watch out!" Those were words of acceptance and admiration.

The old world of Gross Breesen, with the gender restrictions and expectations, began to fade. Eva enthusiastically commented on her new roles:

> *I am much more involved in the work here and also in the farm, than it was the case in Breesen. The reason is probably that I get much closer to everything and through that know more and have a much better overall view. For instance, I am already able to do the harnessing almost on my own and generally it [is] quite different to do the work. One does know why it is and what for. If it were my own land, I would not work and feel differently. I am really happy and satisfied doing it, and I only still miss the Virginia-people* [those selected to come to Virginia who have not arrived] *then everything would be complete.*[112]

Trudi echoed Eva's observation: "The thing that I like so much here is the independence. We do the work which we think to be right, every single one has the responsibility, it is one's own fault if it does not turn out. Everything is almost as if it were their own household, like a large family."[113]

Eva kept a detailed, daily work diary, which was written in English. Every evening after dinner, she sat at her small desk and meticulously penned the work activities of the day. She not only listed what they were, but she also explained why she did what she did. Her learning curve ascended dramatically. In addition to the work diary, she also created a seed label archive, which she kept for the rest of her life.

"The Woods Are Burning!"

Emblazoned in memory were the events of April 10, 1939. In the height of the forest fire season, the day was unusually hot and very windy. Eva wrote in her work diary:

> *The boys wanted to burn a field so that they could disc it. But as the wind changed suddenly, and it was rather warm and dry, the woods started burning. I was just coming out to fetch Howard, when Manfred came and shouted, "Run. The woods are burning." We ran home and everybody rushed out, but it was already too late. We were only nine people, and the fire was burning in a long line through the woods. We started putting it out, beating it with the branches of the pine trees, but it did not do much good. Then we started clearing a path, where the fire should stop. But it went over and we made about three more paths without much positive results. Even plowing did not do much good. The fire stopped at the furrow for a moment, and at the next blow of the wind, it went over. Luckily the ground was rather wet underneath those dry leaves and the trees did not start burning. If they would have started in that wind, it would have been nearly impossible to stop it. After a while, help came. And those people brought the right tools which we did not have. The help was the CCC boys. They made a path about twenty yards off the fire and cleared it of dry leaves and twigs and set another fire. As the two fires met, they had to go out because nothing was left for burning. We very quickly had the fire under control and put it out. Late in the evening, we went out again and put out the smoldering spots. There were quite a lot of them. We mostly covered them with soil. They set the fire on Monday. In Germany, Easter Monday is a holiday; they felt the fire went out of control because they were not supposed to be working.*[114]

Luckily, there were two CCC (Civilian Conservation Corps) camps in the vicinity of Hyde Farmlands, Camp Pershing and Camp Gallion. Each provided extensive training and experience in fighting forest fires, especially developing the cherished and famous "backfire" technique. At the camps, firefighting trucks stood in readiness and were equipped with shovels, picks, rakes and glistening, stainless steel backpack Indian Pumps. There were several fire lookout towers in the area, and because the terrain was relatively flat, smoke from the fire was quickly spotted. On April 10, when the fire raged out of control, the fire unit from Camp Pershing appeared on the scene in what must have seemed to the students a miracle. They were in the vicinity cutting forest roads and building small dams. These were the CCC men who were heroic legends in Virginia.[115] If it had not been for the CCC men of Camp Pershing, disaster would have wiped out the woodlands of Hyde Farmlands and probably destroyed the entire farm.

Preparing meals for larger groups was not so complicated, for at Gross Breesen, the girls cooked for one hundred. Just outside the kitchen, Eva pulled on the bell rope that called the farm workers to lunch, which was the heaviest meal of the day. Lunch consisted primarily of vegetables—cabbage, potatoes, tomatoes, sweet corn, string beans, beets, carrots and onions—and, of course, home-baked bread. Homegrown beans became a staple. Chicken stew and soups were favorites. Canned food was purchased wholesale through the nearby Piedmont Sanitarium in Burkeville, and many of the harvested vegetables grown on the farm were canned. In the summer of 1939, twenty-seven different homegrown vegetables were listed in Eva's diary.

After lunch, there was a short rest period when the *Richmond Times/Dispatch* was read daily. The young people were stunned by what was happening in Europe, especially in Nazi Germany. In the summer of 1939, newspapers clearly mapped out what Germany's intentions were. In August, the students read the front-page story that Germany intended to return the free city of Danzig to the Reich. The Associated Press story stated, "Germany had put finishing touches to 'preparedness' measures."[116] As the students huddled around the newspaper spread on the dining room table, they were grim. Everyone agreed that there was going to be an invasion of Poland. There was no doubt in their minds that war was imminent. It was on a seed purchasing trip to Richmond on September 1 that Eva heard the dreaded news from the newsboy shouting: "Extra! Germany Attacks Poland." War in Europe had begun.

For Eva and her comrades at Hyde Farmlands, a country saying held enormous truth: "A good wind just firms up a young tree's root hold." Life on the farm was demanding, but with each day's labor, muscles were strengthened and spirits buoyed. Of all the emotions running rampant, hope and confidence reigned supreme. The young farmers were setting new roots in American soil. Years later, Eva's daughter, Jacqueline Jacobsohn, wrote these words about her mother and her Hyde Farmlanders: "They had only to stand in their fields, run their hands through their plantings, and gather in their crops. On the knees of their existence, they rise out of the Virginia soil—these young men and women, collecting their lives in the harvest in their hands."

Preparing the fields for planting was the highest priority. The horses and mules pulled plows that disced the earth. It was crucial to develop ways to improve the planting beds and reduce the scourge of erosion. Growing tobacco was profitable, but it depleted the soil of essential nutrients. Everyone cheered when Eva read aloud a poem from the *Extension News* written by the Tennessee Valley Authority:

> *Hordes of gullies now remind us*
> *We should build our lands to stay,*
> *And, departing, leave behind us*
> *Fields that have not washed away;*
> *On the land that's had our toil,*
> *They'll not have to ask the question*
> *"Here's the farm, but where's the Soil?"*

Those who were the first to live at Hyde Farmlands grew to be extremely close. Their purpose in preparing the farm for the refugees yet to arrive was crystal clear. Sharing every aspect of the hard work strengthened their friendship, but for Eva and Ernst, that closeness grew into something more.

Chapter 23

TÖPPER IN EXILE

Töpper was despondent as he left Germany and arrived in England. His family planned to stay there, but after four months, an opportunity for his father moved the family back to Holland in the early summer of 1938. While in England in February, Töpper had met Bondy, who was traveling to New York to meet William B. Thalhimer to discuss the possibilities of the creation of a farm in Virginia. Their reunion was joyous, but Bondy cautioned Töpper not to talk about the new possibility of this American immigration location. There had been so many disappointments that he did not want to add another for the students at Gross Breesen. After all, Thalhimer did not even have a farm at this date. Nevertheless, the two were hopeful. And no matter what, Töpper was elated just to be with his Bo once again.

Töpper learned to love Amsterdam. The rest of his family was involved in work and studies, so he was usually on his own. This, for Töpper, was a wonderful turn of events. Just as he had done when he lived in Berlin, he rode his bike exploring the city, often at night. "As [he] rode along the canals in the moonlight, the streetlights reflected in the water. Most of all, [he] liked to ride to the harbor, where [he] climbed onto one of the wooden posts used for tying up ships. Lit [his] pipe, and enjoyed the nocturnal peace and the view of the boats and water."[117]

No matter how free he was in Amsterdam, he felt he was nothing more than a chess piece strategically placed on the board by an invisible hand that picked him up and placed him where he was, but he had no idea why. He began to sense that history was unfolding all around him, and as he became more interested in current events, he read newspapers and magazines that discussed world affairs. On March 11, 1939, he listened to Radio Luxemburg announce the German annexation of Austria, the Anschluss, when Hitler was welcomed with open arms. The Nazi takeover without any resistance affected him greatly. He realized that Hitler was not going to be stopped. He wrote in his diary: "Things seem to be seething in Germany. Hitler wants to secure his power by terror and threats…He has sinned against the German people! He has debased them to the level of rabble, taken away their sense of beauty and goodness, awakening and inciting in them bad instincts. He enslaves and violates the people, and they love him nonetheless…Hitler is tyrannizing two German countries—who will break the chains?"[118]

All this was occurring while he waited to receive a visa to join other Gross Breeseners at Hyde Farmlands in Virginia. Amsterdam served as a transit base from which other students departed for their new lives or waited for visas. Most important was that the students had left Germany and, for the moment, gained safety. Some students joined the agricultural training center Werkdorf Nieuwesluis at Wieringen, Holland. There, they gained further agricultural training as they awaited the next step to freedom. Every time Gross Breeseners passed through Amsterdam, Töpper met them, and the reunions were always joyous.

One such meeting was particularly poignant. Twenty Gross Breeseners arrived in Holland on June 11, 1939, and were met by a Gross Breesen contingent already at Werkdorf. Bondy flew from Berlin to see them off on the ocean liner *Slamat* of the Rotterdam Lloyd Line, destined for Australia. He received a royal welcome when he stepped off the plane, surrounded by his students, and the excited conversation lasted well into the night. There was no need for a formal farewell speech. Everyone already knew the unspoken words: "We are Breeseners, and we have confidence in each other, in our work and in our will." The students had heard those exact words countless times. The next day, as the group stood together on the wharf, one of the students played his accordion, and all sang a song they had learned years earlier while still in the Bund movement:

> *And remember the far away homeland*
> *For the little troop, it prepares itself greatly*
> *To leave the gray bastion.*
> *And nothing holds us any more,*
> *And we are very happy.*
> *Soon sails will flutter towards the East.*

As the ocean liner pulled away from the dock, the students on the pier waved their white handkerchiefs in unison following Bondy's instructions, as if he were an orchestra conductor: "Up!—Wait!—Down!…Up!—Wait!—Down!" The students on the ship responded with a similarly synchronized handkerchief drill. Because of the improvised flag signals, both parties were kept in sight for a long time until distance blurred the image and made the gestures indistinct. The fellow Breeseners slipped away and turned toward their new lives in Australia.

The departure was so moving and dramatic that it could have easily been a scene in a movie or a piece of fiction, except that it was absolutely real. All the other well-wishers on the dock had departed, but the students and Bondy remained standing silently even after they could no longer discern the waving white flags of their classmates. As they walked from the pier, Töpper could not hold in his true feelings: "Virginia hovers before us like a mirage… it is really only an illusion."[119] As soon as he said it, he felt guilty. He rejoiced in the good fortune of his friends who were escaping, but he could not hide his own dismay. The emotions of elation got all mixed in with the feelings of despair.

Chapter 24

KRYSTALLNACHT, NOVEMBER 9–10, 1938

They have cast fire into thy sanctuary.
—Psalm 74:7

W hat the Breeseners did not know:
What happened on November 9–10 really started on November 7. In the German Embassy in Paris, seventeen-year-old Herschel Grynszpan shot a German official. He really wanted to kill the ambassador, but he was absent from his office. Grynszpan's mind snapped. He could not endure the painful news from his parents, who had been deported back to Poland by the Nazis in late October. Their situation was horrible. The Nazis expelled all Polish Jews out of Germany, and Poland refused to accept them back. The refugees were starving and exhausted. They were caught between two impenetrable walls that had no doors. They were desperate. The wounded German official died on November 9. That was the opportunity for Nazi propaganda minister Goebbels to signal that the most horrific pogrom against the Jews should begin.

In Breslau, Dr. Willy Cohn, a professor, wrote in his daily diary: "November 8, 1938. The newspapers today are reporting terrible news for us. Von Rath, the secretary of the German legation in Paris, was shot by a Polish Jew and severely wounded…[There] will almost certainly have the worst possible consequences for us in Germany. I assume that there will be confiscations, imprisonments…[There] will have dire repercussions for all of us."[120]

The students at Gross Breesen probably did not read the same news story, or if they did, the implications of retaliation did not sink in. They might have listened to the radio station broadcasting in German from France, but they did not have the same historical perspective that Professor Cohn had. Without their knowing it, the two-minute radio silence on all German radio stations memorializing the fallen diplomat punctuated the calm before the storm. They did not know that in the nearby town of Trebnitz, the havoc of the pogrom had already exploded. An old Jewish man, in his nightshirt, was paraded through the streets in chains.[121]

On the evening of November 9 in Breslau, Esther Ascher, a fourteen-year-old Polish-born girl who had escaped the Nazi roundup of Polish Jews on October 18, settled down to the normal after-dinner activities of reading and talking with her brothers. The children went to bed as usual around 10:30 p.m. Suddenly, she was awakened by the sound of shattering glass and loud shouts. "All of us awoke, not knowing what this noise was about. We huddled close to the windows, and finally dared to part the curtains to look down. Below us we saw people ramming wood poles through the showcases of the Jewish store, we heard screaming, and saw people enter the showcases as looting began."[122] It was a known fact that many of those who were smashing the windows of Jewish businesses were teenagers, members of the Nazi youth. The students cheered when a window splintered or a synagogue burned: "*Raus mit den Juden.*" ("Away with the Jews.")[123] The order to attack and destroy Jewish synagogues and businesses was transmitted with precise effectiveness. This was a time when the telephone and the telegraph were the "advanced" means of communication. Ninety-one Jews were killed on Krystallnacht; seventy Jews who were already in concentration camps were murdered during the night of November 8. A total of 191 synagogues were burned, 76 were totally destroyed, cemetery chapels and community centers were torn down and twenty thousand Jewish men were

The smashed storefront windows of Jewish-owned stores throughout Germany on Krystallnacht symbolized the pogrom that shocked the world and the beginning of the "Final Solution." *Courtesy of USHMM 86838.*

arrested, most sent to concentration camps. "The entire nation [was] in uproar."[124]

Esther Ascher did not dare go outside until the next day. She did not look Jewish, so she could mix in with the other Germans without being noticed. She could not believe her eyes in the daylight. It was as if a tornado had hit every Jewish store, vacuumed out the contents and scattered them on the sidewalks and streets. Her curiosity turned to disgust and fear.

Years later, Esther relived the dreadful night:

Sounds That Pierced the Night

Sounds of shattering glass break
The silences of a star filled night

Thunderous voices of vicious thugs
Shouts and shrieks rise from the street
Tearing asunder the peaceful sleep
Of a frightened, fearful family.

Voices swell, wave after wave,
Vicious curses fill the cool air
Penetrate through thin glass of
Windows; shielding for the moment
Lives of a shocked, stunned family
Trembling, questioning their fate.

The sounds of broken glass are surging.
Can there be such abundance of crystal?
Is this the spark that heralds destruction?
An omen, a prelude to shattered lives?
Ensuing silence does not signal serenity—
Shattered glass cannot be restored.[125]

People all over the world learned what had happened overnight. A telegram dated November 10, 1938, was sent to the U.S. secretary of state by Ambassador Wilson from Berlin. The contents of the report were bone chilling:

> *In the early hours of this morning systematic breaking of the Jewish owned shop windows throughout the Reich and the burning of the principal synagogues in Berlin was carried out. Observers noted no uniforms of Nazi organizations among the perpetrators of this action. Nevertheless, it is not conceivable that this admirable body of police would have tolerated such infraction of order unless general instructions to that effect had been issued...the Consulate in Breslau reports arrests of Jews there this morning.*[126]

The terror of Krystallnacht began on November 9. That date was of particular significance to the emerging Nazi historical narrative. It was on November 9, 1923, that Hitler led the failed Beer Hall

Putsch, an attempt to overthrow the Bavarian government. Nazis were killed and, in Hitler's mind, martyred. He spent the next year imprisoned, and during these solitary days, he wrote his seething anti-Semitic *Mein Kampf* ("My Struggle"). Added to the humiliation of defeat, the Nazis traced the birth of the hated Weimar Republic to the German revolution's victory on November 9, 1918. All the pent-up frustration and anger were unleashed on November 9, 1938; this date was stamped in history by the indelible, polished boot print of the Third Reich.

There was now no way to deny that the pogrom was planned and held ready for the opportune moment. It was as if the fates had determined this calendar of destruction. Von Rath died on November 9. When Hitler heard that violence against the Jews had already broken out, he ordered that the assaults should not be halted and that the police should be withdrawn. "The Jews should get the feel of popular anger."[127]

Eva's classmates in St. Paul's read the *Evening Standard*, an outstanding British newspaper, on November 10. Not knowing that she had already left Berlin, they feared for her safety: "The trouble began when half-drunk mobs armed with crow bars and bricks began window-smashing…[and] mishandling Jews and placarding shops with handbills…the handbills read: Fuhrer! Free us from the Jewish plague!"[128]

In Richmond, Virginia, William B. Thalhimer sat at the breakfast table and opened his daily *Times/Dispatch*. He and his wife, Annette, looked at each other with dread. They both remembered the fear they had felt in 1930, when they experienced a rally of the Brown Shirt Nazis. Thalhimer immediately focused on his new friend Curt Bondy and the young students at Gross Breesen.

GROSS BREESEN, NOVEMBER 10, 1938

The day was gray, but the cold winds of winter had not as yet arrived. In the morning, Dr. Bondy left the grounds for a dentist appointment in Breslau. As he drove into the city limits, he saw the devastation. He asked what had happened, and upon hearing the news of the pogrom, he turned around and sped back to the campus. Just as he arrived, so did the Gestapo. All the students and staff were lined up in the courtyard, and their names were being called off from typewritten lists. Students and staff were separated first by the boys from the girls. Then those males eighteen and above formed a second group. After everyone was accounted for, the older students and staff were ordered onto the gray trucks at the point of rifles. There was no talking; fear paralyzed any show of emotion. Helpless students stood at attention as they watched their friends and teachers prepare to depart. The trucks revved their motors and drove off. No one knew where they were heading, but all feared that a concentration camp was their final destination. None, including the staff, knew what had happened all over Germany during the previous night and the present day. The telephone lines had been cut. After the trucks departed, the younger students were imprisoned in barns where soldiers stood guard outside the locked doors. Then the fury of Krystallnacht was set loose on the manor house. It was

On a surprise Gestapo raid on Gross Breesen on Krystallnacht, the younger students were imprisoned overnight in the horse barn. *Courtesy of the* Circular Letters.

as if a deranged, rabid police dog was unleashed and commanded to rip to shreds anything in its path.

Gestapo and local farmers, including Gamoth, the resident blacksmith, ran into the castle and "vented their 'spontaneous' rage on the furniture."[129] Cupboards were overturned, and dishes and glasses crashed onto the floor. The grand piano, the pride of Bondy and Eva, was hacked into splinters by axes and sledgehammers. The taut wire strings of the soundboard whined as they snapped and flew into the air. Chairs were thrown through windows, doors were reduced to splinters. The wooden cabinet housing the holy Torah scroll was crushed. The Torah's velvet covering was ripped off, the silver ornamentations were pocketed and the Torah itself was carried to the dung pile, where its ancient parchment sections were ripped into pieces and thrown onto the steaming manure. That was the ultimate desecration. The statue of Michelangelo's David was beheaded with one swift swipe of a two-by-four. Axes, hammers, crowbars and clubs tore into every corner of the castle. The orgy of destruction lasted for an hour. Its fury culminated with the exhausted celebration of a drinking fest in Bondy's room by the Gestapo officers.[130] The violent outburst against the Schloss was perhaps more than just anti-Semitic rage. It was also a retaliation by the peasant workers who lived on the farm against the aristocracy that had ruled their lives for hundreds of years. The have-nots saw the destruction of the house as a fitting spit in the eye of the landed gentry. Not all the Aryan farmers approved of such brutality, and they did not participate in the frenzy; but some did. The illusion of safety and peace that enclosed Gross Breesen proved to be just another Jewish glass window destroyed on Krystallnacht. The sense of security was shattered forever.[131]

The Gestapo trucks drove south toward Breslau. In complete silence, the students were dazed with confusion and fear, and the staff felt nothing less than terror. They knew the capability of Nazi torture. As they approached Breslau, smoke could be seen from the burning synagogues. The air smelled of the pungent odor of ash. The students were stunned by the events of the day as they filed into the police jail for an overnight stay. There, they gazed at other prisoners whose faces and clothing were scabbed with dried egg and

On Krystallnacht, the Nazis burned and destroyed Jewish community centers, cemeteries and synagogues. Firemen protected neighboring buildings but allowed synagogues to be destroyed. *Courtesy of USHMM 23609.*

blood. The students did not have to ask what cruel humiliation the men had endured. That night, the students were fed, and no physical harm came to them. Their personal belongings were collected and precisely catalogued. The next day, they learned that they would be transported to Buchenwald Concentration Camp near the city of Weimer. Their thoughts doubled back to Gross Breesen and their concern for those left behind, but they also cringed as they considered the ordeal that was certain to come.

Chapter 25

IMPRISONED IN BUCHENWALD CONCENTRATION CAMP

The Gross Breeseners, along with over two thousand Jewish men from the Breslau area, boarded a passenger train at the Breslau station on the morning of November 11. In the background was the panorama of a smoldering city and a broken community. For the students, whatever semblance of peace and security they had felt in the past two years was quickly demolished. The madness was about to begin.

Ernst Cramer, a popular teacher and assistant to Bondy, recalled what happened when the train reached Weimer:

> *The whole horrible episode began at the train station, in a tunnel under the tracks. We—several hundred Jews from Silesia—had been transported in a special train to Weimar. With ear-splitting shouts, uniformed guards threw us out of the compartments and drove us through the underpass, beating us indiscriminately with sticks.*
>
> *After a while, we were forced through the deserted square in front of the station into waiting trucks. After a short drive, they beat and chased us again, mockingly, this time through a much too narrow gate, over piles of rocks purposely put there, and into the camp.*

FROM NAZI GERMANY TO THALHIMER'S FARM

After having stood at attention for hours on the sodden, muddy assembly grounds, the guards assigned us to five recently built wooden barracks through which the wind blew. A total of 2,000 people lived in each building, none of which had windows or doors, only an opening in the middle. Bunk beds five beds high and less than a foot-and-a-half wide stood nailed together. The only way to reach one of these wooden plank beds was by crawling.

There were no blankets, sinks or sanitary installations. The latrine was still being dug. Nobody was given any water. Some people lost their minds that first night.

I remembered the stand on which people were beaten. I saw before me the gallows, from which a prisoner swung.[132]

The students were physically and emotionally exhausted. The hours of standing at attention in precise lines was torture. They continually tried to gain a glimpse of their beloved Dr. Bondy. They feared that he would not be able to withstand the extreme strain. The students had been hardened by being constantly outdoors and working through the discomforts of cold and rain. They were in excellent physical condition, but the men standing next to them were not farmers, not accustomed to being exposed to inclement weather. They suffered a terrible shock to their bodies. Orders were barked to proceed to the unfinished barracks named "Operation—Jews." Those Jews rounded up on November 10–11 were segregated from the other prisoners. In all, there were approximately ten thousand Operation Jews occupying five barracks, two thousand per building. Soon after imprisonment, each man's hair and beard were shaved. The twenty Gross Breeseners knew one another extremely well, but after each had been shaved, they sometimes did not even recognize one another. Head shaving was just one of the ways the Nazis tried to dehumanize the captives and strip each of his individual identity. The aggressive punishment was particularly intense in the first few days of incarceration. The Nazis wanted to break the spirit of the prisoners quickly. Bondy wrote:

The prisoners had to sit for hours around two whipping racks and watch while various captives were flogged with different

A roll call of the thousands of imprisoned Jewish men over the age of eighteen at Buchenwald after Krystallnacht. On arrival, their heads were shaved to demean the prisoners. *Courtesy of USHMM 79914.*

kinds of whips. During one of the first nights the storm troopers were permitted to vent their rage freely. Water was distributed in the night after a long period without any beverage. I suppose that a laxative was mixed in the water. The poor chaps who then ran out of the barracks were pitilessly tortured, shot at, strangled, and mistreated in other ways. I cannot guess how many captives died in that horrible night, but it was a considerable number.[133]

One of Töpper's closest friends and roommate, Prinz, experienced the wrath of the Gestapo officer SS sergeant Zoellner. Prinz had turned around to look at another Breesener. That was strictly forbidden, so the sergeant, with the sharp edge of the leather heel of his boot, stomped on the student's foot and ankle with all his force. Luckily, Prinz had his work boots on, and the repeated blows did not penetrate. Zoellner repeatedly slammed his boot onto Prinz, but he did not show any sign of pain. This frustrated the Nazi officer and he lost interest, for "it was not fun anymore."[134]

Within the special camp, the prisoners could walk about freely during the day. This allowed the Gross Breeseners to find one another and stick together. Those who were not at Gross Breesen during the roundup and picked up outside the campus joined their old friends. Being able to band together fortified the students. No one felt so alone and vulnerable. They were stunned, however, at what Bondy experienced immediately. He broke down. He cried uncontrollably in spasms of remorse. He felt that all the trust the parents had placed in his hands had been destroyed. He did not fear for himself but for his "boys." The students tried to console him, but they were unable to calm his broken spirit. Within a few hours, however, Bondy regained his composure. One could actually observe him returning from the depths of desperation. He was once again the calm, observant Bo. The boys were relieved.

The nights held the greatest terrors. Police dogs barked wildly, and screams shot through the darkness. The "laundry room" also served as a sick bay. Twenty to thirty prisoners died daily from sickness, malnutrition or the lack of needed and accustomed medications. Old people were the most vulnerable. The latrine was nothing more than a giant pit with logs stretched across it. Waiting one's turn in a group to use the latrine was agony. Two prisoners actually fell into the pit and drowned in the sewage. No matter where one was in the camp, he could hear the announcements coming from the loudspeaker. Incessantly, throughout the day and into the sleep-deprived night, the loudspeaker played a tactical, intimidating role. For all sorts of reasons, the camp officers called out the names of prisoners or delivered orders for the general camp. In the morning, roll call was a central activity during which absolutely no talking was permitted. The process of just getting out of the barracks took hours. Chaos was the norm.

As a psychologist, Bondy observed the total breakdown of civilized behavior. "The urge of self-preservation, bestial fear, hunger, and thirst led to a complete transformation of the majority of the prisoners. The ruthless struggle of 'each against all' began. No one spoke in ordinary tones; every one screamed. The main thing was to get something to eat and to drink. When food was brought in, an excitement ensued which one can otherwise observe only among animals."[135] Prisoners displayed the worst of human behavior. What remained was a "wild, ruthless, and thoroughly senseless struggle for individual survival. Every trace of reason disappeared." Many inmates were driven insane or committed suicide by "severing an artery or running into the electrically charged barbed wire."[136]

When Bondy observed his students, he realized that they behaved in ways that were completely opposite from the majority of the other prisoners. They never lost their sense of responsibility to one another, and they did not panic. "From the beginning, they set themselves the goal of bringing their entire group out of the concentration camp without loss of life or breakdown of nerves... without having suffered serious illness or loss of sanity."[137]

But something else happened in the camp. The name "Gross Breesen" became a rallying point for other prisoners as well. The students observed intense misery all around them, but they would not be consumed by it. Instead of retreating into their own protective shells, they turned outward to the rest of the incarcerated. They ministered to the other inmates who were suffering and demoralized. Some gave up their own food rations; others accompanied the elderly to the latrine. They dispersed their own spirit of hope and strength as if it were precious medicine smuggled past the guards and the barbed-wire fences. They became living testimonials to "human dignity, determination and courage." Through their ministering to others, they found the strength to survive. Bondy knew that his efforts to teach life lessons had taken hold. Now, more than ever before, he was certain that Gross Breesen was more than just a place, a school, a period of time in the lives of teenagers. Gross Breesen was an attitude, a spirit, a set of values to live by. Because of what he saw in his students, he once more could believe that there was a future.

Chapter 26
PANIC AND RESPONSE

The horrific events of Krystallnacht were reported from embassies, consulates and international reporters. News of the Nazi pogrom spread like the dreaded Black Death. The world was stunned. No one knew for certain what was happening inside the concentration camps in Germany, and for those not left on campus at Gross Breesen, no one knew exactly who had been imprisoned. Not knowing led to panic, and within the turmoil of Krystallnacht, communication broke down.

IN HOLLAND

The first news of Krystallnacht reached Töpper on November 10 through Dutch radio and newspapers. He learned that twenty-four Gross Breesen students plus staff were imprisoned in Buchenwald Concentration Camp, but he did not know all their names.[138] He was terrified for his friends and his beloved Bo. He felt so helpless. Immediately, he and a friend from Gross Breesen, Meui, who was living in Amsterdam and spoke fluent Dutch, went to the Jewish Committee in Amsterdam. Töpper hoped that if the Dutch Jewish Committee sent a guarantee of entry permits for the imprisoned Breeseners to the German authorities, release from Buchenwald would be attained sooner rather than later.

When he arrived at the headquarters, he was shocked by the chaos of hundreds of refugees pushing their way to enter the overflowing building to talk with an official inside. "Many had tears in their eyes, others paced back and forth in the square wringing their hands, desperation written on their faces. All had relatives or friends in Germany who had been arrested and whom they wanted to help get out."[139] Töpper had never seen such anguish.

The building was a maze of offices and corridors. After the two talked their way through the front door, Meui took the lead because he spoke Dutch and most of the other petitioners did not. Calmly, and with a sense of authority, he confronted various officials sitting at desks in the hallways, and finally, the two found the office of the two people who would be of the greatest help. They knocked on the closed door, and without permission, the teenagers entered the room. Sitting at desks were Rudolf Elk and Gertrude van Tijn. Meui "presented [their] request calmly, succinctly, and with impressive resolve. Elk and van Tijn listened attentively."[140] Töpper realized that he was too emotional to earn the attention of the officials. He marveled at how mature his friend appeared and how controlled he was. He was certain that such an attitude caught the immediate sympathy and approval of the Jewish Committee. This was the first step to free his friends. He was terrified that nothing would help, but he knew he had to try.

In the back of Töpper's mind were the imagined scenes of his friends being brutalized by their Nazi captors. Getting the Breeseners released as quickly as possible was his first goal. His father supported his efforts and gave him money for telegrams and expensive long-distance telephone calls. Communication was dreadfully slow. In addition, telephone conversations to Germany ran the risk of being tapped by German intelligence, and letters from Europe to America took weeks. First, Töpper needed to procure the names of those in Buchenwald, and he had to secure funds to give to the Dutch authorities to cover the expenses of supporting the refugees in transit camps. He reasoned correctly that before the German authorities would release prisoners, they had to have evidence that the Breeseners in Buchenwald had Dutch entry permits and were also awaiting immigration visas.

Töpper sent urgent telegrams to the United States. Time seemed to drag in slow motion. He could not sleep at night and became irritable. Phone calls to Germany did not supply the needed information because everyone was afraid to speak. The two weeks after Krystallnacht dragged on, but then there was a breakthrough.

Töpper finally obtained the list of all the prisoners from Gross Breesen and also the list of those designated to immigrate to Thalhimer's farm in Virginia. The financial guarantees to pay for the work camp in Holland were telegrammed from New York and presented to the Dutch authorities.

In America

William B. Thalhimer was shocked by the reporting of the devastation and imprisonment of German Jews. His first thoughts focused on Dr. Bondy and the students whom he hoped to welcome at Hyde Farmlands. It had already been almost seven months since he purchased the farm and began negotiations with the State Department. He called the head of the visa division, Avra Warren, a person with whom he had developed a trusting, personal relationship. His questions were frantic: What did Warren know? Did he have a communication from Raymond Geist, the consul general in Berlin? Did he know if Bondy was imprisoned along with how many students? What would happen to them in a concentration camp?

Thalhimer's calls to the State Department and to officials dealing with Jewish refugees in New York City soon gave him terrifying answers to his questions: Bondy and Gross Breesen students, most of whom were on the list to immigrate to Virginia, were imprisoned in Buchenwald. Efforts were initiated to contact the Dutch and the U.S. consulate in Berlin, but Thalhimer was frustrated as several more weeks passed. Being unable to help wore him down.[141]

Chapter 27

RELEASE FROM
BUCHENWALD

T he news that Töpper had been waiting for so feverishly arrived. He was delirious. On December 6, 1938, he wrote in his diary: "Fantastic! In the morning came a telegram to the effect that all boys, except Bo and Scheier and four more, have been released."[142] Then came a telegram sent to a friend of Bondy's in Amsterdam: "Everyone returned healthy from trip. Please inform my brother immediately."[143] Bondy called the concentration camp ordeal "a trip." He did not want to aggravate the Nazi censors and cause additional trouble. A similar telegram was sent from Geist, dated December 10, to the State Department:

> *December 10, 9 a.m.*
> *Continuing my November 26, 10 a.m.* [telegram] *Curt Bondy with 24 students and additional instructors in Jewish Agricultural School Breslau arrested and placed in Buchenwald concentration camp. All except Bondy and other instructors and two students released. Have sent Bondy letter requesting him to call here. He intends to apply for no quota visa.*[144]

Thalhimer was informed of the good news by the State Department. Finally, after almost a month of desperation, all of the Gross Breeseners were released along with most of the 2,100 Breslau men rounded up on November 9–10.

Two men in Germany—Fritz Schwarzchild and Martin Gerson, both German Jews and connected to Gross Breesen's governing board—convinced the Nazis that the Breseeners in Buchenwald were eligible for entry permits to Holland and were being considered for immigration into the United States. This letter was crucial in gaining their release. Töpper's efforts paid inestimable dividends.

The released students traveled back to Breslau and reported to the Gestapo headquarters to receive the valuables that had been confiscated on their way to Buchenwald. They were amazed at the accurate record keeping of the Gestapo as they returned their belongings. The Jewish community of Breslau fed the students and celebrated their freedom. The ordeal at Buchenwald was over, but it would never be erased from the memories of those who experienced the nightmare. As they left the concentration camp, they were advised never to discuss what happened, and if they did, they would be immediately imprisoned "for life." They were ordered by the Gestapo to leave the country and never return. That order was especially cruel because it ignored the most pressing question: Where could the students go? Eventually, every member of the "first generation" of Gross Breesen would find safety scattered all over the world.

On December 17, a rainy day, on Shabbat evening, the students and Bondy lit the first candle of Hanukkah. The dark memories of Buchenwald and the Krystallnacht raid blackened the room even more as the lights in the room were shut off. As the students sang "Ma'oz Tzur" ("Stronghold of Rock"), they lit the candles of the Hanukkah menorah. The candle flames, which recounted the victory of the ancient Maccabees, reflected off the tired faces of the students who had come face to face with Nazi evil. Now they were hopeful but not entirely confident. Hanukkah, the celebration of freedom, deliverance and rededication, took on an entirely new relevance in their lives. Some of the more religiously knowledgeable students recited the Birkat Hagomel, the prayer of thankful deliverance.

When Töpper met his friends in Amsterdam after they were released and on their way to the Dutch agricultural work camp, they were all in good physical condition, though noticeably thinner. He could hardly recognize them because their heads were still shaven. They needed quiet time to recuperate, and they were unexpectedly silent. Even though they were outside Germany, they still did not feel comfortable revealing the details of their ordeal. The fear inflicted by Nazi mind control lingered. The students still suffered from the traumatic stress of Buchenwald. It would take time before they felt whole and secure again.[145]

Back in Richmond, Virginia, Thalhimer was greatly relieved. He continued his efforts to convince the State Department to grant visas to the students on his list as the stranglehold on U.S. visas began to loosen. Bondy was assured a visa through his sponsor, the College of William and Mary, to teach at Richmond Professional College in Richmond. However, he did not leave Germany immediately after his release. He returned to Gross Breesen to pick up the pieces and arrange for a new director of the school.

As the new year of 1939 was approaching, Töpper wrote to Bondy from Holland:

> *It has been a long and trying struggle, a year of waiting, a year tumultuous and rough. For you personally the year ended with a blow. You sowed Virginia and reaped Buchenwald. And both are more than names, more than a destination or an experience. They are symbols...Last year we hoped for a year of accomplishments. This time I can really wish us only* **courage and hope** [emphasis this author's]*; let that be the spirit in which to enter the New Year.*[146]

Chapter 28

THALHIMER'S VICTORY!

No one connected to Gross Breesen, not the students or even the staff, really understood what William B. Thalhimer did from April 1938 to May 1939. The students knew of Thalhimer's "Virginia Plan," but they did not have the faintest idea of the tireless work and commitment that was invested on their behalf over the year that it took for Thalhimer and his lead lawyer, Leroy Cohen, to win visas for the students and staff. What started out as a low-priority request from Thalhimer to the State Department ended up achieving the close attention and, ultimately, decisions made in the highest offices of the secretary of state and the secretary of labor. At first, Thalhimer did not have a chance to succeed, for there was outright resistance and animosity toward him and his plan to purchase a central Virginia farm for German Jewish refugees and turn it over to the Gross Breesen students and staff. The State Department had done everything it could to restrict immigration in the 1930s. Instead of issuing the allowable 26,000 visas for immigrants from Germany per year, the department granted only 4,000. That meant that through administrative red tape, from 1930 to 1938, instead of 208,000 visas being issued, only 32,000 were. In addition, there was no immigration category designated as "refugee." Lurking behind the scenes was the fact that there was blatant anti-Semitism in America and at the highest levels of the government. Thalhimer surveyed the immigration terrain and concluded that it was a topography of exclusion. But he would not give up. He devised a plan to issue shares to the students so they could eventually own the corporation farm. He had a "fire-in-the-belly" obsession to save the young students and ensure their safety in America. For thirteen months, he waged battle after battle against the aggressive, bureaucratic hostility of the State Department. Few people can even imagine Thalhimer's enormous courage and hope. The Richmond benefactor never lost his composure; he never lost the goal of rescue from Nazi Germany.

Finally, on May 23, 1939, thirteen months after he purchased the farm in Burkeville, a crucially important meeting took place with the State Department and the Labor Department, one that would finalize the outcome of all of Thalhimer's efforts, either positively or negatively. Everything was riding on the outcome of this meeting.[147] After over a year of meetings, memos from Washington to Berlin and back, letters and legal rulings, discussions and interviews and arguments between the State and Labor Departments, it all came down to a firm handshake between Thalhimer and the State Department. Thalhimer had won over the hearts and trust of those who had to make the final decision to grant visas. The hard-fought battle to scale the granite and "paper walls" of the State Department, the frustration and the worry that had consumed Thalhimer and Leroy Cohen for so many months concluded in victory. A key sentence in a State Department memo said it all: "Inasmuch as Mr. Thalhimer is a responsible citizen and merchant in Richmond and is an officer on the resettlement committee for Jewish refugees in the United States, it was agreed that his assurance of support would be sufficient to meet the requirements of the law in each particular alien's case."[148]

Thalhimer, Cohen and Harold Young, a Washington lawyer who was part of the negotiating team, walked out of the State Department and paused on the concrete sidewalk in front of the massive building. They were afraid to even smile for fear that what had just happened was only a mirage. But they could not contain their elation any longer. They could not believe that they had won the battle. David had defeated Goliath. They had dreamed of this outcome, but they never dared to admit that they might fail. They had lived and breathed their efforts for what seemed forever. Their handshakes and hugs cemented an effort that was gigantic. There were still more hoops to jump through because each candidate for a visa had to be interviewed by the American consuls in Germany, Holland and England, which is where the students on the Virginia list were living. The Gross Breeseners were not on Virginia soil yet, but the way was now cleared for their fateful journey to begin. On the drive home from Washington, D.C., to Richmond, Thalhimer's buoyant mood seemed to float the car right off the pavement, flying home to tell Mrs. Thalhimer the spectacular news.

Chapter 29

WAITING FOR A VISA

The released prisoners of Buchenwald received Dutch visas to attend the transit work camp. There, along with 250 young people, most of whom were headed to Palestine to settle on kibbutzim, the students continued to learn agricultural skills. Töpper gained permission to join his friends, even though he could have lived with his parents in Amsterdam. The Gross Breeseners bunked together, and their spirits were high. The usual adolescent banter was crisp and often downright humorous, a throwback to the Bund days of their younger years. They all chipped in to purchase a radio for the dorm so they could keep up with world affairs and listen to classical music. The routine of work on the farm included dairying, haying and tending to the crops. Learning to farm picked up where their training at Gross Breesen ended.

"RETROSPECTION AND PROSPECTS"

It was the tradition in the Gross Breesen *Rundbriefe* (*Circular Letters*) to write an analysis and evaluation of the passing year as the new year approached. Bondy asked Töpper to partner with him in the writing that would be sent to the Breesetners who were now scattered all over the world. Students received the letters from Bondy and responded with reports of their own. The *Circular Letters* became the lifeline by which the spirit and experience of Gross Breesen were kept alive and friends could keep in touch. (Today, the equivalent of such a letter writing system would be some form of the Internet's social media.) As the prospect of a Gross Breesen community immigrating together was no longer possible, Bondy wrote:

> *Every one of us has to search for his specific task and his specific aim. But to all is the farming vocation, which has to be the real vocation and fulfillment. Equally common is the personal attitude: decent, frank, courageous and helpful, people who want to lead a full and intensive life…In reality, it is as it is, to live, to fulfill the tasks set for everybody, to meaningfully organize every day, That is our task.*[149]

Bondy was realistic. The dream of transplanting the Gross Breesen community as a colony in another country could not materialize. The new home that he talked about would be the one within each of his students. There would never again be a Gross Breesen place, but there would always be a Gross Breesen spirit and bond that would allow the students to be home with themselves, wherever they settled. Bondy's initial faith in Töpper, from their very first meeting, proved itself to be true. Obviously, Bondy recognized something very special in his student. He wrote:

> *I think that there is no sense in mourning for the old Gross Breesen now. Look, that would be the same as if people leaving their youth were to mourn continually for that time, as if their values were irretrievably lost. People who understand how to live know very well that when they grow up, the experiences of their youth represent an important and essential component of their existence as adults. Gross Breesen was preparation and a time of youth; The Gross Breeseners in Argentina, in Virginia, in Australia, in Kenya, in Parana should represent real and good adult life and confirmation of it. Töpper, my friend, isn't that enough for a life's goal, do we have any reason to be sad and lose hope?*[150]

Always encouraging and clarifying experience, Bondy focused on what Töpper had done to bring about enormous good effects in helping his fellow students emigrate from Germany to Holland. "You yourself have no reason at all to complain about lack of plans and of courage. We know very well how much you have worked and accomplished for Gross Breesen just recently. So, the new year will be full of important, good, and fulfilling tasks for us Gross Breeseners."[151]

Chapter 30

TÖPPER'S JOURNEY TO HYDE FARMLANDS

As an entry in the *Rundbriefe* written in July 1939 from Gross Breesen, Ernst Cramer wrote: "Accept a last greeting now from us [future] Virginians from the old Gross Breesen. In the next *Circular*, we, as well, will be able to report from our work abroad. Hopefully the people from Holland and England will also be in Hyde Farmlands already."

While living in Holland, Töpper witnessed the immigration of his friends, but he still was not cleared to receive a visa for himself. He anxiously hoped with all his heart that he would not be left behind. Holland was still a neutral country, but it did not take a crystal ball to conclude that Hitler's Nazi armies would eventually invade western Europe. It was as if the entire continent was a frozen pond, and with every heavy Nazi step, Europe's surface-ice cracked and echoed with ice thunder. It was a scary time. War with Germany was postponed through the negotiations of appeasement between Hitler and Lord Chamberlain, but history never looks upon appeasement favorably, and this was no exception. Chamberlain's "success" proved to be a failure when Germany invaded Poland on September 1, 1939. England and France, which had signed a treaty with Poland, declared war on Germany, but they did not engage Germany, as yet. When the students already at Hyde Farmlands read of the invasion of Poland, they feared the worst for their fellow classmates at Gross Breesen. Would they escape the Nazis once the onslaught spread?

After what seemed an interminable, frantic wait, Töpper was summoned to the consulate in Rotterdam in the last week of September 1939. The consulate had been notified that he was on Thalhimer's Virginia list. It was a nerve-racking experience, and so much was riding on the decision to grant him a visa. His affidavit of financial support in America was finally cleared. The questions at the interview seemed outlandish, but he had to take them seriously: "Have you been a Communist? Do you want to murder the President of the United States? Have you been jailed?"[152] The physical examination on October 3 found Töpper to be in fine health, so all was now settled. He was granted a U.S. visa.

On October 29, Töpper stood at the railroad station and waited for the train to Antwerp. His family and a few friends gathered around him. His younger brother, Hans, then eleven, cried. Töpper, who was now nineteen, wrote in his diary: "My baggage had gone a few days earlier and was now on the ship. My parents tried hard to smile as they hugged me. With a pounding heart I got on the train and waved to them from the window. It was the last time I saw my father, standing by the car, waving to me."[153]

Töpper tried to hold back his tears, but he couldn't. He wondered if he would ever see his family again. He tightly held onto the new typewriter his parents had given him. He was an avid writer; he would use the typewriter for years to come writing a diary that chronicled his life experiences.

At dockside, he gaped at the size of the *Veendam*, the ocean liner that would carry him to his new life in freedom. With a black hull, white decks and two orange smokestacks with black and white bands, the ship dramatically awaited its human cargo. Coincidentally, this was the same shipping company that one year before had carried Eva and her sister to New York. The ship flew the flag of Holland that was brightly illuminated at night to signal German U-boats that it belonged to a neutral nation. The submarines crisscrossed the North Atlantic like a pack of deadly, torpedoing sharks. Unlike when Eva sailed, the ship was overcrowded, especially in Töpper's third class. Americans wishing to return home and refugees fleeing Europe quadrupled the number of passengers. Once aboard, people were almost giddy from relief, for just booking passage was nearly impossible as the war spread.

The ship did not point its bow onto the open Atlantic for a couple of days. First, there was a stopover in England, and it was there that Töpper nearly lost his visa. Looking back, it seems comical, but when it was happening, it was deadly serious. In Southampton, British naval and immigration officials came aboard to review the ship's manifest. Töpper stood in a roped-off area witnessing a commotion among the officials. He could not understand what they were saying. They were looking for an unaccounted passenger. Suddenly, Töpper's friend grabbed him by the elbow and led him to the interrogation room. Much to Töpper's astonishment, the immigration officials had been looking for him for half an hour. His German passport was not stamped with the customary red "J" that signified that the holder was a Jew. The officials asked serious questions: Was Töpper a German who was trying to enter the United States for some unknown reason? Perhaps to spy? Fortunately, a member of the crew listened to the questioning, which was not going well. He saw that Töpper understood very little and was anxious. The crewman explained that Töpper had been at the transit Jewish work camp in Holland, and only Jews were at that camp. He was certainly a German Jew. His passport had been issued before the Jew stamp became law. The aggressive tone of the interrogators changed to one of calm relief. If Töpper had not been able to have his passport explained, he would have been labeled an "enemy alien" and jailed in England. The *Veendam* would have sailed without him.[154]

Like all the other Gross Breeseners who crossed the Atlantic, the journey for Töpper was filled with paradoxes. It was both a forced exodus and a welcomed rescue; it was sad and joyous; it was a looking backward and into the future. The emotions ran the gamut, but Töpper and his newly made friends experienced the crossing more as an adventure. Because the seas were often stormy, the teenagers ate more than their share when others were confined to their cabins. Teenage boys have the capacity to consume mounds of food.

The *Veendam* arrived in New Jersey, where Töpper's anxiety peaked once again. He could not understand what the officials were saying. Words swarmed into a gibberish buzz. The other passengers had people to meet them, and when this happened, their faces turned from worry to relief. Not so for Töpper. How would he maneuver getting off the ship if he could not understand the immigration officials, and even if he did, where would he go? After what seemed an eternity, Joseph Loewensberg, the elder brother of Breesen staff member Ernst Loewensberg, arrived to rescue him.

Joseph led Töpper on a thorough, introductory tour of New York City. Everything seemed like a dream. He met people at the Joint Distribution Committee, those who helped him procure a visa, but he could not converse in English. He could not relate how grateful he was except to the German-speaking Ingrid Warburg, a member of the famous Warburg family, who had visited Hyde Farmlands with Bondy in 1938. After six days in the city, Töpper boarded an overnight Greyhound Bus heading for Richmond, Virginia, where he was going to meet William B. Thalhimer at his office in the department store. The ticket cost eight dollars. The bus's route south wove through city neighborhoods, shore towns and country villages surrounded by farms and forests. Compared to Holland and Germany, America seemed immense and full of startling contrasts.

It was still night as the bus approached Richmond, and the anticipation of meeting the man whose name was held so dear increased. What would William B. Thalhimer be like? Would he be welcoming? The bus arrived at the station as dawn was breaking, long before stores opened and sidewalks became crowded with people hurriedly walking to work.

After storing his luggage in the station, Töpper walked the streets, anxiously looking at his watch, waiting for Thalhimer's Department Store to open. When the large square clock above the entrance pointed to nine o'clock, the door was swung open by the uniformed attendant. Töpper entered the store and was amazed. It looked exactly like an upscale department store in Berlin. He really did not know what to expect, but he was impressed.

He approached a saleswoman and, in a heavy German accent, haltingly asked where Mr. Thalhimer's office was. The young

Töpper looked for the famous square clock of Thalhimer's Department Store before meeting William B. Thalhimer. *Courtesy of the Thalhimer family archives.*

woman "stared at [him] as if he were some kind of creature from a fairy tale, and then began to giggle and apparently told one of her colleagues that this boy wanted to see the 'big boss.'"[155] After several inquiries, someone finally took him seriously and escorted him to

William B. Thalhimer, in his store office, greeted many of the Gross Breesen refugees as they traveled to Hyde Farmlands. *Courtesy of the Thalhimer family archives.*

the top floor by elevator. A secretary knocked on Thalhimer's office door and announced Töpper's arrival. Thalhimer stood up from his chair, came from behind his large desk, grasped Töpper's hand and smiled deeply. He was genuinely excited to welcome another Gross Breesen student. Töpper was greatly relieved. It was hard for him to comprehend that he was actually standing in Thalhimer's office and that he was shaking the firm hand of the man who engineered the Virginia Plan.

Thalhimer was fifty-five, short and balding, but he exuded purposive energy and confidence. He reminded Töpper of Bondy, but he was more open and jovial. He had that "American smile." After a short chat, which Töpper could hardly understand, Thalhimer put his arm around his shoulder and proudly introduced him to the secretaries in the large office.

Töpper returned to the bus station and boarded the bus to Burkeville. The ride took several hours as it slowly made its way into what seemed an entirely different country. In the *Rundbriefe*, he had read Ernst Loewensberg's early report from Hyde Farmlands many times. He had memorized the landmarks, and sure enough, from the large bus window, everything he had imagined about Virginia came to life. There were gentle hills of hay pastures, vegetable gardens that had been turned over in late autumn, tobacco fields, small farms everywhere, dirt roads and forests. The bus driver called out "Burkeville, next stop." Töpper's pulse was racing. He wondered who would meet him at the station. As the bus turned off the main road, he saw a red farm truck parked near the single pump in front

The red farm truck became a symbol of new life and industry at Hyde Farmlands. *Courtesy of the Eva Loew collection.*

of the gas station. Standing next to the running board was a smiling young man, a farmer in overalls. The two waved.

After a hearty handshake and a back-slapping hug, Töpper threw his suitcase onto the flat bed and climbed into the cab. The truck bounced over the potholes of the parking lot and then turned on to Old Plank Road heading south toward Hyde Farmlands. Töpper was all eyes and talking in German. It all felt so familiar and right.

The flatbed was built to carry heavy loads, so its commercial springs buffeted the passengers as if they were riding bucking broncos. It did not matter to Töpper. He could not wait to drive up the long gravel driveway and embrace his Breesen friends once again, but this time on American soil.

Töpper was one of the late arrivals to Hyde Farmlands. A small mob ran from wherever they were to surround him, hug him and lead him into the main house. They all but carried him on their shoulders. Many had not seen him since he suddenly left Gross Breesen. Reality was beginning to set in; he was finally at Hyde Farmlands. He walked through the main house and admired the rooms, especially the library with its wood stove, bookshelves and upright piano. Eva stood on the fringe of the crowd. She smiled as their eyes met. The welcome was all that he had hoped for after his long waiting and journey. He did not have to imagine any more; reality pinched him. He could not stop smiling.

Chapter 31

TÖPPER AT HYDE
FARMLANDS, 1939–1940

Töpper remembered his nightmares when living under the Nazis. His life at Gross Breesen liberated his spirit, and his years in Holland matured him, even though he always felt he was living in exile. At Hyde Farmlands, he began another chapter in his life. He was overjoyed to be with Breeseners again, but the farm and the surrounding countryside took on a meaning and dimension that was different from the others and totally his own.

Töpper was a dreamer, a romantic who saw the dense woods encircling the farm as a playground for adventure. Others saw the forest as raw materials for building new structures or potential fields and pastures once the land was cleared. Töpper peered into the dark woods and imagined wild animals to hunt and fantasized savages to stalk. Others saw workhorses to harness for the plow or wagon, but Töpper's mind could envision them as galloping stallions carrying him to some mysterious grotto. He soon planted one foot in the busy schedule of work on the farm, but the other foot tiptoed into a world of exciting possibilities. All the western adventure novels he read as a teenager, especially those of Karl May, now came alive, and he was determined to live a new life that had previously been deprived of boyish freedom. Now he envisioned himself as a pioneer, a settler in an untamed and Apache-threatened new world far from Nazi tyranny.

Töpper confidently drives the horse and wagon at Hyde Farmlands. *Courtesy of the Eva Loew collection.*

He purchased a Winchester rifle from Sears & Roebuck and a German shepherd that he named Bingo. His fantasy of becoming a hunter was rapidly obliterated as his "hunting" excursions became near disasters. He shot trees more than squirrels. He soon realized that the idea of hunting was more exciting than actually pulling the trigger and coming face to face with the death of a living thing. Any aspiration he might have had to become a serious hunter quickly evaporated.

Horseback riding was another matter. Eva and Ernst rode trail horses, but Töpper had to settle for the workhorses. Any riding he did came after a long day's work, for the humans as well as for the horses, which were not remotely motivated to entertain a "cow boy."

Nevertheless, Töpper learned to ride bareback, and stealing the horses out of the barn under the cover of night added to the adventure of riding in moonlight. In truth, Töpper did not so much ride the horse as the horse led and tolerated him. He often dropped the reins, and the horse, knowing the way back to the barn, proceeded as if under autopilot. These escapades ended with his being discovered and rebuked for such "childish behavior." Even Dr. Bondy scolded

Töpper, the "hunter." *Courtesy of the Eva Loew collection.*

him in a letter sent from Holland. Töpper admitted that some of the criticisms were justified, but they did not affect him. As he wrote later, "After all, I had just spent five years of my youth, from the age of 12 to 17, under Nazi rule, with my daily life, as a Jew, increasingly restricted. I wasn't going to curb my enjoyment of this new freedom."[156]

EXPLORING THE COUNTRYSIDE

Töpper ecstatically explored the countryside. Severe gullies folded into themselves and eventually descended to a flowing creek that tumbled over an alluring waterfall. This spot became one of his favorites when he needed to cool off after working in the hot sun. He first dangled his feet in the cool water, and then he undressed and washed himself under the falls. This was such a relief from the stifling summer heat of central Virginia. The woodland was home to a long list of animals and birds. At supper, the students reported their sightings and compared notes: brilliant red cardinals; pileated woodpeckers; huge, soaring turkey vultures; hawks; wild turkeys; hummingbirds; raccoons, foxes and deer; opossums; and even an occasional bobcat or bear. The large black snakes unnerved the uninitiated Europeans. The only snakes they had ever seen were in the Berlin Zoo. One such snake made its way into the main house and was promptly killed. Its skin was presented to Thalhimer as a trophy on one of his visits. Needless to say, its six feet of length never made it into the Thalhimer home.

TÖPPER'S STRAWBERRIES

Töpper was appointed the "Director of the Department of Small Fruit." This grandiose title meant that he was a committee of one to plant and grow strawberries. He had to prepare the soil, plant, weed and water the plot. One day, he decided to enlist the help of Lu and Rowdy, the farm's mules, to pull the cultivator in between the rows of strawberries. The idea was a good one, but it failed miserably. Lu and Rowdy sensed Töpper's disdain for them, so they did everything to thwart his project. They pulled out of control and stomped through the young plants. Then they began to run, dragging the cultivator on its side and scraping away plants and soil. Töpper lost complete composure. He ran after the mules, cursing their names, until they settled down at their barn. He disliked mules before, but now he became a lifelong hater of these beasts of burden. Long arguments were sparked occasionally at mealtime: which was the better work animal, the horse or the mule? People took sides as if they were engaged in hot political arguments. Much to Töpper's dismay, his roommate, George, drove the mule team in his excavating sand out of the creek beds for cinder block fabrication. He never had any trouble with the mules, even though one had the reputation of killing a man with a lethal kick. But one has to wonder who was more stubborn: the mules or Töpper?

THE SLAVE QUARTERS

With more people coming to live on the farm, dormitory space was at a premium. With two of his close friends from Gross Breesen, George and Prinz, Töpper decided to live in the slave quarters located behind the kitchen of the main building. Every building on the farm was historical, some dating back to the 1750s, when it was a land grant by the king of England. Its evolution to a large southern plantation, with over sixty slaves noted in the 1860 census, caught the imaginations of the young farmers. Living in slave quarters had special meaning for these refugees who had fled their own kind of slavery in Nazi Germany. Previously, the building had been used to store corn, grain and feed. A stone cooking fireplace heated the small cabin. It was especially cozy in the colder months as the heat rose to the sleeping platform above. Even though it no longer was a granary, rats, acting out of habit, visited their old hangout. That did not deter the new human residents, though the sound of scratching rat claws caused many a restless slumber.

Often when Töpper walked through the doorway of the cabin, sat before the open fire or climbed the ladder steps to the sleeping platform, he felt an indefinable presence. He wondered what it was like to be a slave before the Civil War or a black man living in Jim Crow country. He remembered vividly when William B. Thalhimer visited the farm and addressed the students on the shaded front lawn of the main house. "Learning How to Live in the South" was the topic for the day's talk. Speaking in a light southern accent, Thalhimer clearly wanted the students to understand the mores of living in Virginia, for he did not want anyone to get into trouble with the locals for not knowing how to act toward black people. He wanted to explain "how it was." In his address, he referred to the blacks as "Negrahs." He presented a hypothetical situation that exemplified the response that he urged all the students to adopt: "If one were driving the farm truck and saw a black person hitchhiking, he could stop to pick him up, but the 'negrah' could not sit up front in the cab of the truck. He would have to sit outside on the flat bed." He continued by pointing out that the white students should address the black man by his first name or by calling him "uncle" and should never use the term "mister" or use his last name, even if he knew it. It took Töpper a while to realize that Thalhimer spoke to the students to safeguard both the immigrants and black Americans. If the Klan caught a white man sitting next to a black man in the cab of the truck, both could have suffered injury, or worse. Racism was alive and well in central Virginia.[157]

As a refugee who had escaped from Nazi Germany, Töpper was particularly sensitive to racial discrimination. His first face-to-face encounter with a black man occurred while the two worked in one of the chicken houses. He was troubled:

> *Several days long we sat facing each other in one of the henhouses and cleaned eggs for shipment. After he had noticed that I behaved towards him differently than he was used to from Whites, and after I, in broken English, had told him something of my past, he gained confidence and told me something about his own life. He was an older man, the grandson of a slave, and from his very carefully formulated report I could get an idea of what it meant for someone like him and his family to live in a Southern state in the USA…and I, a Jew who had emigrated from Germany, was quietly ashamed to be a white person.*[158]

TRIPS TO CREWE

Short visits to the neighboring towns broke the routine of hard work. The red farm truck served as the bus that transported the young people to nearby Crewe. Neighbors smiled and waved to the passengers who sat on the flat bed. Often, the joy of getting a break from work burst into song and laughter. Attending movies was a treat. The most remembered was *Gone with the Wind*; it was so long that the students had to return a second day to see the end of the movie. Töpper was so impressed by the story that it became the first book he read in English, struggling with the help of an English-German dictionary.

Crewe was a bustling small town with ice cream parlors, a pool hall (off-limits for the girls) and drug-, hardware and small department

Business Section, Crewe, Virginia

The students loved the ice cream counter at Crittenden's Drug Store in Crewe, Virginia, when they took a break from the daily routine on the farm. *Courtesy of Robert Flippen.*

stores. On the weekends, the town's population swelled with the farmers from the area and the CCC men from nearby camps. For some inexplicable reason, the students loved to watch the enclosed delivery wagon pull out of the icehouse yard as it dripped a trail of melting ice on the hot roads. Maybe it reminded them of the cool watermelon treats and pit-spitting contests enjoyed on the farm.

In the 1930s, Crewe was a major railroad hub. Its roundhouse was an engineering wonder of great interest. Because the steam engines could not drive in reverse, they rolled onto a huge turntable that rotated the engines in order to face them in the direction from which they came.

The two small clothing and shoe stores were owned by Jews, the Machts and the Beckers, who welcomed the refugees into their homes on the Sabbath and on religious holidays. When Eva visited the Machts, she was delighted to see the mezuzah affixed to their front door. With bittersweet memories, it reminded her of home.

THE BLIZZARD OF 1940

On January 24, 1940, Virginia was buried by the biggest blizzard since 1899. The winds blew the snow into drifts as high as twenty feet. The entire state was marooned for a week, and Hyde Farmlands was totally cut off from the rest of the world. The muffled snow silence soothed the hearts and minds of the young refugees. The sharp realities of their lives were softened by the graceful swirls of the rounded snow mounds that covered everything, including barns and sheds. After shoveling paths and tunnels through the drifts to attend to the animals, the students were liberated to play snow games. Afterward, when they entered the main house, the warmth invited a cherished sleepiness that triggered childhood memories of playing in the snow and coming inside for hot chocolate. Germany and family seemed so far away and long ago. Being snowbound was strangely numbing, mixing joy with the melancholy of vanished images from the past. Eva recollected winter ski vacations with her family in Switzerland, and Töpper remembered snowball fights and sledding with his friends. The past was the past, but it seemed so alive.

Ernst Loewensberg rode for the mail and supplies during the record-breaking blizzard of 1940. *Courtesy of the Eva Loew collection.*

Chapter 32

MAJOR CONSTRUCTION AND A CHICKEN INDUSTRY

The decision was made that Hyde Farmlands needed to shift its efforts from farming and growing tobacco to the production of chickens and eggs. This was a safer form of farming because its success did not depend on the vagaries of weather and soil quality. In order to do this, ten large log chicken coops and two cinder block brooder buildings had to be built. The construction project began by conferring with the Extension Service agents in the search for suitable designs. Because he had been a skilled woodworker at Gross Breesen, Hermann Kiwi became the overall project manager. The construction project was huge and complicated. The students were divided into work crews. One team cut down the straight pine trees. Two-man saws chewed into the soft wood, and axes lopped off the branches. The rhythmic sounds of *chunk* and *thud* echoed with each axe blow as forest roads were cleared to allow the horse team to drag the trees out of the woods. Driving the horses was difficult and dangerous. The trunks were dragged to the area where the Oliver-powered buzz saw was positioned. They were lifted by hand onto a platform where they were cut to the desired lengths. The saw screamed and trembled as it tore through the bark and heartwood. The large, exposed circular blade with razor-sharp teeth was a scary piece of equipment, seemingly alive and ravenous. Those

Harvesting timber for the chicken coop construction. Using the two-man saw are George Landecker (right) and Manfred Lindauer. *Courtesy of the Eva Loew collection.*

The construction of the brooder house in 1939–40 from handmade cinder blocks was a massive accomplishment. *Courtesy of the Eva Loew collection.*

Making cinder blocks for the brooder house was labor intensive. Notice the famous Wizard block maker. *Courtesy of the Eva Loew collection.*

who operated the saw were constantly reminded that just one unintended slip could tragically culminate with a severed hand. The cut logs were lifted onto sawhorses, and the peelers stripped the bark with their drawknives, exposing the shiny, moist, yellow-brown pulp. There was a slow learning curve for the uninitiated. Töpper tried his hand, but he soon learned that debarking is more a matter of finesse than that of strength or speed. He needed to slow down. He had to learn that the drawknife stroke involves a releasing backward before slicing forward. This technique harbored a broader life lesson—forward progress often entails stepping backward first—but that insight was not readily absorbed by youthful enthusiasm. Before the log walls of the coops were raised, concrete floors were poured on a crushed stone foundation. The ten large chicken houses were located on a well-drained, southern-exposed slope east of the main house in order to capture as much sunlight and heat as possible, especially needed during the winter months. A line of trees sheltered the coops from westerly winter winds. While crews worked on the chicken houses, the construction of two cinder block brooder houses began.

Cinder Block Construction

Töpper was a member of the team that made cinder blocks. He worked for hours with his hoe mixing the carefully measured sand, ash, water and cement in a wheelbarrow and then poured the block mixture into the rectangular cast-iron forms of the famous Sears & Roebuck Wizard. At first, he and his teammates gawked at this odd-looking contraption, which had earned an outstanding reputation for efficiency and durability. It was featured in the *Sears Catalogue*, which, at the time, was the most widely read "book" in America. Töpper never considered himself very mechanical, but this machine earned his admiration. He lifted the pressed concrete forms from the Wizard and placed them nearby to dry in the sun. He made thousands of these blocks, but for some reason, the horses considered them as intrusions into their territory, objects of scorn. After their day's work of plowing, they ambled over to the drying field and diabolically stomped on as many blocks as possible. Töpper and his fellow laborers were enraged. He cursed the horses

Ten chicken coops were constructed from the plans provided by the Virginia Extension Service. Even after seventy-five years, some still remain. *Courtesy of the Eva Loew collection.*

and chased them away. Understandably, the workers quickly fenced in the drying field.

Once the brooder houses were outfitted with incubators, the celebration of this enormous completed building project commenced with well-earned jubilation. Building permanent structures where there were none before buoyed the spirits of the refugees. Before, at Gross Breesen and Hyde Farmlands, buildings were refurbished, but now, the students were not just improving what was preexistent. Starting from scratch, with hard labor, they planned and constructed substantial structures. In reality, they became accomplished contractors. The sense of a new beginning was palpable. Hyde Farmlands was becoming their own new home, their own future. Pride of accomplishment was a welcomed tonic for these displaced persons, and how pleased they were when neighbors, visitors and particularly William Thalhimer praised their fine workmanship.[159]

Chapter 33

CONSTANT WORRY

Around the table at breakfast, lunch and dinner, the students read and discussed the newspaper articles and maps of the worsening situation in Europe. Often, Eva read the papers aloud to the others, and she frequently had to translate from English into German. The headlines of the *Times-Dispatch* on May 8, 1940, were worrisome: "Dutch Forces on War Footing" and "Germans Reported Moving on Holland." On May 10: "Nazis Invade Holland." Those students who had emigrated from Holland just a few months earlier struggled to comprehend their luck. Tragically, not all of the Gross Breesen students who were living in the transit camps in Holland got out in time. Everyone was worried that Bondy might be caught in the Nazi blitzkrieg that hammered western Europe. They did not know if he had escaped from Amsterdam in time to flee south into France.

Töpper's family was trapped in Amsterdam when the invasion commenced, and not hearing anything from them was maddening. At the end of every one of his diary entries between May 10 and June 24, 1940, he wrote: "No news"…"Still no news"…"When will I get mail from my parents? I could go crazy!"[160]

Ten days after the German invasion of Holland, Hyde Farmlands was hit by a severe rainstorm accompanied by thunder and lightning. Töpper went out at night into the storm and walked in the buffeting winds. The dark sky was slashed by bolts of lightning that illuminated the fields. The chaos of the storm mirrored the unbridled pain that he felt: "It is horrendous, glow worms, lightning and rain. Fantastic. No news from Europe. War situation unclear, apparently more German advances in the heart of France. The Germans? The Nazis! But, unfortunately also the Germans."[161] The feelings of helplessness and betrayal, accompanied by guilt, drove the young people into quiet anguish. The raging storm of the natural world that night reflected the affairs of man, as if a grand Shakespearean tragedy descended on Burkeville. Every day, news of the war fatigued the students with worry for family, friends and their beloved Bo. They could do nothing to prevent the catastrophic events that wore down their optimism. Especially for those who had been imprisoned in Buchenwald, they could do little to outrun the invisible phantoms that stalked them or silence the desperate voices of their families that called to them in their sleep.

No one knew if Dr. Bondy was safe. If only he could join his students at Hyde Farmlands.

BONDY'S ESCAPE

On May 9, Bondy was in Brussels working on plans for two hundred young people to immigrate to San Domingo.[162] There, he heard the first bombs dropped on Brussels as the Nazi invasion began. When he tried to return to Amsterdam, he found that all the northbound trains had stopped running. The only escape route was south into France. The train never reached Paris; he was stuck for three days and three nights without being allowed to disembark. On his way south, after weeks of close calls, he was incarcerated in an internment camp. After several days, because he held a San Domingo passport, he was released and made his way to Lisbon, Portugal. On August 10, exactly three months to the day of the German invasion of Holland, he sailed to America with a U.S. non-quota visa as a professor. Thalhimer's friend John Stuart Bryan, president of the College of William and Mary, arranged for Bondy to become a faculty member of Richmond Professional Institute, a division of the College of William and Mary. When the students at Hyde Farmlands learned that Bondy had landed safely in New York on August 21, they were elated, and his arrival at the farm was anticipated with joy and relief. The news was exactly what the students needed.

After a welcoming celebration of gratitude that Bondy had rejoined his beloved students, it became evident that "Herr Professor" had changed. The endless toil of trying to rescue young people and his own internments in Buchenwald and France had sapped much of his energy. His escape exhausted him. He was a tired man, not broken, but not the same. The aura of self-assured leadership, the spirit that had inspired and molded his Gross Breesen wards, was diminished. It would take time to regain his strength and energy.

Chapter 34

HYDE FARMLANDS CLOSES, 1941

As 1940 turned into 1941, life on the farm became more productive and promising. Ernst Cramer, a Bondy assistant at Gross Breesen, was selected as the new overall administrator, and George Landecker, Töpper's roommate, became the farm manager. Large-scale chicken farming was developing rapidly. Some refugees had been on the farm for two and a half years; they were the ones who saw the greatest changes in the makeup of the community and the overall progress of development. They had experienced the electrification of the farm in 1939, a giant leap into modern life that most of the neighboring farmers saw as nothing short of miraculous. They appreciated the water tower that brought running water and showers into the main house.

Hyde Farmlands experienced growing pains. To the disappointment of many, it did not become a second Gross Breesen, for several reasons. First, of crucial significance, the students were older and each had a different vision for the farm and for his own future. Nineteen- and twenty-year-olds are very different from those who are fifteen and sixteen. Second, the farm's population had grown to thirty, too large for the farm to support and too diverse. Not all the farm inhabitants had experienced Gross Breesen and therefore did not have the Breesen "attitude." Furthermore, for most of the farm's life, Curt Bondy was still in Holland; the absence of his leadership and guiding spirit was keenly felt.

Despite all these complications, cooperation and commitment to the farm's success continued. Those who loved farming thrived and could see themselves as farmers in the future. According to the extension officials, the farm was well on its way to becoming the most modern chicken operation in Virginia, the gold standard for the future.

Closing

In early 1941, optimism was dealt a death knell. William B. Thalhimer was again stricken with heart disease and hospitalized. That news shocked many in Richmond and everyone at Hyde Farmlands. Those who relied on him for his leadership in the national resettlement of German Jewish refugees felt an urgent sense of uneasiness. Letters of concern poured in from all over the country. The painful news rocked the Hyde Farmlanders with questions about the future of the farm.

It wasn't only poor health that preyed on Thalhimer. He reluctantly concluded, along with his cousin Morton, that the farm was in trouble financially. It was quite simple: there were too many people living on it, and even though great progress had been made, the farm was not yet self-sustaining, and that would not be accomplished for several years. He also acknowledged that future immigration to Hyde Farmlands was frozen. By 1941, the gates of emigration from Germany and immigration into America were welded shut. His goal of making Hyde Farmlands an ongoing training institute for refugees had to be abandoned.

An evening meeting on February 12 was called by Curt Bondy. In his typical, straightforward manner, he did not sugarcoat the situation: sooner or later, the farm would be dissolved, and the young men and women would soon be contemplating their next moves. On February 14, the final decision was made. The farm would be broken up immediately and sold. The young farmers listened to

FROM NAZI GERMANY TO THALHIMER'S FARM

Bondy's words in intense quiet. Töpper wrote in his diary, "The group, and me too, acted in a strange way. With lots of resentful remarks and some anxiety."[163] In truth, he projected onto the others his own uneasiness more than how the rest actually felt. To their credit, the pervasive attitude was one of acceptance and a desire to "move on." Morton Thalhimer and Bondy made sure that every member of the farm community had a viable place to go after the farm disbanded.

Between late February and early spring, the students departed to all parts of the country. Thalhimer's farm rescued them, gave them some breathing time and now served as a springboard from which to launch the students onto the next trajectory of their lives. They were at another crossroads, another dislocation, another beginning that would require immense energy, but most were ready. Bondy attempted to fortify them with reality talk about what it would mean to be an immigrant again:

> We are not able to alter the external circumstances under which we have to live. We are not able to alter fundamentally suspicion of strangers, the economic and political conditions, hate of Germans and anti-Semitism....No one is politically more powerless than the immigrant...We have to make ourselves aware of our general and special situation with complete clarity, have to comprehend what it means to be uprooted, isolated and alien, i.e. to be an immigrant.

He urged his students to prepare themselves for the difficulties ahead by being aware of the dangers: "There is no other way, and if one does not have this clarity, one will again and again react to every fresh attack against oneself or generally against Jews and aliens with depression, despondency and desperation."[164]

Finally, Bondy spelled out the future goals each needed to accomplish:

> The individuals will now have to prove themselves in the life out there, they have to learn a lot yet, have to master the language better and have to try much harder to enter in the American lifestyle. The task, which we had set ourselves, to do the groundwork for further Jewish young people from

Europe who wanted to become farmers, cannot at present be continued...Perhaps no other common task arises any more... We will have to shape our life, each one by himself.[165]

William Thalhimer wrote Bondy even as he was recuperating: "I feel like a father towards all the boys and girls at Hyde Farmlands and will always be ready to give them whatever counsel and advice they may need. As time goes on, questions will always arise and I know you will feel free to call on me."[166]

Packing was not complicated, for most had few possessions. The books in the library were divided among those who wanted certain volumes, and the piano, which brought music and a touch of the old Gross Breesen atmosphere, remained in the house for Franken, the new owner. The young men and women sifted through their belongings and gleaned what to throw away and what to keep. It was emotional when they nostalgically fondled objects and photographs. Most of the students' meager possessions had been brought over from Germany, Holland or England. Memories of

For her entire lifetime, Eva kept her original trunk that carried her possessions over continents. Notice the "E.J." for Eva Jacobsohn. *Courtesy of Jacqueline Jacobsohn.*

An emotional, sad day at Hyde Farmlands in 1941. Töpper (on the truck) and Manfred Lindauer load the discarded belongings for the dump. *Courtesy of the Eva Loew collection.*

transit and dislocation mingled with flashbacks of more recent events on the farm. Photographs that had been stuffed into drawers were gently pasted into scrapbooks. Diaries were safely tucked away. Both Eva and Töpper were avid diary writers. Eva, in particular, saved everything, including her report cards from Germany and England, and her photograph album became an extensive archive, as did her farm work diary. She carefully packed the trunk that had traveled with her from Berlin to London, from Berlin to Zurich, to New York, to Cuba, to Hyde Farmlands.

With the inducement of earning a monthly paycheck and becoming a U.S. citizen, Töpper joined the army. Before he was to report for training, he stayed on to put the farm in order. In the last entry of his writing about Hyde Farmlands, he captured the last few days when students resided on the farm. In the voice of the "boy," he revealed his resignation and melancholy:

> *In front of the large house at the back porch stands the "red truck" and a boy is filling it up...The* [truck's] *load is full,*

now it goes to the garbage dump...Everything is splendidly green. Everywhere in the forest and in the park it blossoms, the air is warm, almost too warm already and while driving past, the boy sees that the cherry trees have already come out in buds...The "Red one" [the farm truck] *rattles a bit! Well, tomorrow it will be sold, that doesn't matter any more. So, here is the garbage dump...So, now to drive onto the heap backwards and down with the rubbish. Piece after piece flies...the old iron, the empty food cans and semi-solid butter milk tubs. Now and then the boy hesitates when something familiar comes to hand. But only a moment, then it flies downwards too. There, Otto's arch supports, Prinz's hat, one of Martin's old shoes, Inge's dress belt. Whatever it might be, it all meets again down below, mercilessly. Peacefully united lie the small possessions of so many boys and girls, and the garbage dump does not ask, whether their owners would have been pleased if they had been thrown together in the same way as their belongings now. As the last item, one single sock follows marked 158. Surely a Werkdorfer. Today is the last day, tomorrow he already sleeps elsewhere and nonetheless it was "a home."*

Inside it is empty. Only bits of paper and scraps of dust are lying on the floor. No furniture any more, no pictures. The walls look bare and ugly now, everything is so dusty and dirty. One can tell that for several days no girl has been in the house...The boys have no time to clean up.

He goes once more through the whole house, to see whether he has not forgotten anything...the few remaining items are put aside and then the place is swept. "Farewell celebration!"...the boy sweeps from the window towards the door. Only in the center, he carefully sweeps around a pile of hand luggage. It's his own... Actually, it was a beautiful dream! But now it is finished! How does one frequently say? I see, of course. Finality! [167]

Töpper sat on the edge of the flat bed after he pushed the discarded possessions and garbage onto the dump heap behind the chicken coops. He looked into the darkness of the surrounding woods and down the dirt path that led to the stone foundation of the old abandoned mill. The day's light was waning, and the birds sang softly, with lingering pauses between songs. Night was approaching. He hunched over from fatigue and melded into the hush. He was pensive. Endings were everywhere. His mind wandered back to his first day at Hyde Farmlands. Scenes of his exploring occupied most of his thinking; how he loved to explore and discover nature, but he had the feeling that all the disruptions and dislocations in his life had begun to accumulate and congeal into questions: Why had he been so moody so often? Why didn't he read the newspapers more and learn more English? Why didn't Hyde Farmlands become a second Gross Breesen? And finally, the biggest question of all: Did he really want to be a farmer?

Töpper was growing up. He gradually realized that before there can be answers, there have to be honest questions. He remembered when he had the same insights at Gross Breesen. As he prepared to enter the army, he wrote to an old friend: "I am afraid of the future, that is quite clear to me. I will overcome this fear or be destroyed by it…Next month I will be twenty-one. My life will probably change. I don't know what will become of me. I only know one thing: there is no taking it easy for me, there is no time without fighting, no time without longing."[168]

The letter was signed "Töpper," but his name would soon change, as would he.

Chapter 35

"TOM," THE WAR YEARS

On May 7, 1941, Töpper and his friend Red reported to the induction center in Richmond. Bondy accompanied the two and wished them well, and as he drove off, the thought that he was entering a whole new life dawned on Töpper.

The official administering the army induction test asked Töpper, "What do they call you?" He hesitated and thought to himself, "What do people call me? Werner? Töpper?" He paused and finally responded, "Tom." At that moment, he realized that "Töpper" was a name reserved for those in his past, from the Bund, Gross Breesen and Hyde Farmlands. When he had applied for the first papers leading to U.S. citizenship a year before in Crewe, he changed his name from Werner Karl Angress to Werner Thomas Angress. He reasoned that "Thomas," and especially "Tom," sounded more like his new American self. Not surprisingly, he greatly admired Mark Twain's Tom Sawyer, so his new initial, "T," could stand for both Tom and Töpper.[169] Starting on the very first day he was sworn into the military, the people he met for the rest of his life called him Tom Angress, but those who knew him from before affectionately called him Töpper.

When the sergeant placed the test paper in front of him, he detected Tom's anxiety and confusion. His English was very limited.

With great empathy, he provided "clues" for Tom to select the correct answers. Without this coaching, Tom never would have been accepted into the army. This was the first of many others who helped Tom become a soldier. Several officers and fellow GIs adopted him, mentored him and taught him English, and Tom was a quick learner. Why did they do this? Tom was small, his face was youthful and he had an accent. He could have been an object of bullying, but he wasn't. Tom was likable. Most called him "Tommy." His smile was infectious. Often, small people have immense energy to make up for their lack of brawn; that was Tom, but despite his small frame, he was also very strong, a direct result of his training and work at Gross Breesen and Hyde Farmlands. He worked hard and trained hard. Four men—Barnes, Jackson, Wilkins and Jennings—took him under their wings. They put him through a crash course in English immersion. Within a few months, he could speak much better, and his reading and writing improved greatly. Rapidly, the army Americanized him as Hyde Farmlands had not.[170]

After basic training in the 116th Infantry Regiment, 29th Virginia National Guard Division, which drew its members mainly from the Lynchburg, Virginia area, he was traveling to Camp Meade in Maryland after the first major maneuver in North Carolina. The soldiers rode in trucks, packed in on bench seats. There was a chill in the air, and the canvas top did not keep out the cold. It was December 7, 1941. That night, while sitting comfortably around a warming campfire, a soldier ran to the group and shouted the shocking news:

Tom Angress, a very proud soldier in the U.S. Army. *Courtesy of the Angress family collection.*

the Japanese had attacked Pearl Harbor. The next day, Congress declared war on Japan, and a few days later, on December 11, Germany and Italy declared war on the United States. America's involvement in World War II had begun. Tom's plan of being in the army for a short time was blown out of the water with the bombs that sunk much of the Pacific fleet.

The monotony and boredom of training exercises and maneuvers stretched on endlessly, from 1941 to 1943. This included patrolling the Outer Banks in an effort to spot German submarines just off the coast. Tom bristled under what he considered military nonsense, but he kept his disdain for unreasonable authority to himself. He was mastering the emotional outbursts that had gotten him into trouble when he was younger. He proved himself as a promising soldier, so much so that he was promoted to the rank of sergeant, specializing in company communications.

THE RITCHIE BOYS

All this changed one day when he read a notice from division headquarters asking anyone who had foreign language proficiency to apply for the next training course at the Military Intelligence Training Center (MITC) at Camp Ritchie in order to become POW interrogators, propagandists, translators or interpreters. The army was in need of German-speaking soldiers as the invasion of Europe was approaching. Tom was accepted and reported to Camp Ritchie, which was near the Civil War battlefield at Gettysburg, Pennsylvania. At Ritchie, he found a new comfort zone and purpose, for many of the soldiers were German Jewish refugees like himself. This was a sophisticated and accomplished bunch. It differed from his previous infantry company where many of the soldiers came from Virginia's mills and some could hardly read or write. At Ritchie, on the other hand, the man sleeping next to him was Fred Hechinger, who later became the education editor of the *New York Times*. The three-month training session, September through December 1943, prepared Tom to be a member of the FID, or field interrogation detachment.

These intelligence soldiers would be attached to various regiments for the battles ahead. It was during his training at Ritchie that Tom received his citizenship papers on October 5, 1943. He had reached another milestone. He was elated. Several other Gross Breesen and Hyde Farmlanders were also "Ritchie Boys."[171]

THE EUROPEAN CAMPAIGN

Preparation for the invasion of Europe on D-Day found thousands of soldiers shipped to England, from where the landing into France was to occur. In England, Tom was attached to the 82nd Airborne Division, and specifically the 508th Parachute Infantry Regiment. These assault soldiers had undergone extensive training, so Tom thought it odd that he was so assigned. He had never been trained to jump, and the promised quick course to teach him was delayed until it was almost too late. D-Day in early June 1944 was rapidly approaching, and Tom was informed that he would not be able to jump with his team because he had not undergone parachute training. In Tom's mind, there was no way that he was not going to stay with his unit, so he immediately ran to the office of Major General James M. Gavin to request permission to jump. This was an audacious act, especially because he went over the head of his commanding officer. Gavin listened to Tom, obviously admiring the intense loyalty he had to his company. Although it's hard to imagine his reasoning, Gavin gave Tom permission to jump in the invasion even though he had not received prior training. In the excitement of immediately returning to the hangar where he would receive inside instruction, Tom never second-guessed what he had done. Youthful courage and hope flowed in the adrenaline rush that certainly blurred his rational judgment. His natural sense of adventure, loyalty and a need to prove himself overpowered any other consideration.

After a day's delay, D-Day exploded onto the beaches and into the air space above France. The C-47 transport plane *Son of the Beach*, with a picture of Donald Duck in bathing trunks painted on the fuselage, flew over the English Channel to France. After only jumping off a seven-foot box as his "training," Tom parachuted safely with his team behind enemy lines. As he floated downward, he felt no terror; he descended with curious detachment. He was exhilarated by the feeling of floating in a silence never experienced before, and miraculously, he landed safely. Many of his fellow jumpers were not so lucky. Of the 2,056 troopers of the 508th Parachute Infantry Regiment who jumped on D-Day, 1,161 were wounded and 307 killed.[172] Tom probably did not know it at the time, but his previous infantry regiment, the 116th Regiment of the 29th Virginia National Guard, stormed Omaha Beach in the first wave of assault. The casualties were enormous. If Tom had stayed with his previous unit, he may not have survived the slaughter.

As so often occurred, jumpers were separated from their units, and that's what happened to Tom. After a few days, he and several others were captured by German soldiers. After two weeks of being a prisoner of war, the advancing American troops overran the Germans and freed Tom and the other soldiers near Cherbourg. While they were captives, the Americans were treated humanely by their German captors and kept safe from incoming American shelling. All during that time, Tom did not divulge that he spoke German. He even played chess with one of the key German interrogating officers. When the Americans were released, his fellow soldiers urged Tom to reveal to the German officer that he understood everything the Germans had been saying while they were prisoners of war. Tom refused and later explained: "From beginning to end he [the German officer] had treated us with decency, and I wanted to spare him what undoubtedly would have been a humiliating experience. Instead I walked up to him and expressed my hope—in English—that the Americans would treat him with the same courtesy as he had treated us. We shook hands and parted."[173] Tom acted as a *mensch* (a decent human being). That was a birthday present he gave himself, for he turned twenty-four on June 27, the very day of his own liberation. He probably did not know it then, but the Jewish plea from the *Pirke Avot* applied to him: "In a place where there are no men, strive to be a man."

From D-Day to the Battle of the Bulge, Tom Angress was in the midst of the fight to defeat Germany. He was wounded and received the Purple Heart and the Bronze Star. He huddled in foxholes and shivered in the intense cold. He was most often dirty and hungry. The Battle of the Bulge was "the most stressful and difficult eight weeks of [his] career as a soldier."[174] Because he was with the FID, he had considerable freedom to move to different locations. Wherever there was a need to communicate with the enemy, especially during the negotiations of surrendering, he played a vital role. He always treated German prisoners with respect, and when he interrogated them, he never yelled at them. Because of his success, he was promoted to master sergeant. He was well known, and his self-confidence flourished. He wrote, "My buddies in the intelligence section often made fun of me by calling me a 'Heinie' and asking, 'Hey, Tommy, how many German war bonds have you gotten lately?'"[175]

As Tom entered Germany in May and the crushing defeat of Germany was approaching, he heard of Hitler's suicide, and along with the others, he toasted, "Long may he rot."[176]

DEATH CAMPS

Up to this time, Tom did not know of the Nazi "Final Solution." He had never heard the name Auschwitz. But all that changed. As the army advanced, his unit stumbled on an abandoned concentration camp named Wobbelin. What he learned and witnessed sickened him. He wrote to Bondy, who, in turn, released the letter to the *Times-Dispatch.* It was printed in that paper on June 4, 1945. The title of the article was "A Sergeant Writes Dr. Bondy of Mass Burial of Internees in Germany":

> *Today we buried the dead that we found in the concentration camp right outside of our town. We buried them in the public square of the town, right opposite the castle of the Grand Duke, and the whole population as well as the captured German generals and high ranking officers had to attend.*
>
> *But before I go into details I would like to tell you a few words about the concentration camp. We found it outside of the town,*

alongside the road, in a wood clearing. It is just a small camp, with about 10 buildings behind the usual barbed wire, and it housed from 200 to 300 slave laborers. The sight was the most horrible one I have ever seen. The place was filthy and smelled of decay, of dead bodies, and foul turnips; gnawed-on turnips were lying around on the barrack floors, in addition to the filth and dead bodies of the inmates. You found them all over the place; piled up, head to feet; in the latrine, in the so-called wash room, in the barrack corners. Two hundred of them lay there, unburied, simply starved to death. Their limbs partly fallen off their bodies already, were as thin as sticks. It was a repulsing, sickening sight. Their bodies were shrunk, only bones and skin. And over a thousand more bodies were being dug out of mass graves by the German population right then, while I was up there. But six kilometers away were people living in a town as good as you can imagine, a bit rationed but not suffering, in nice houses, with dogs and cats that had to be fed and with good clothes to wear. I found several survivors in the camp yet, and talked with them. They still wore their striped suits, they looked more dead than alive, and their faces regardless of age, looked old. They showed me their numbers which were tattooed to the arms, they told me of their suffering. And even if they had not done so, the sight out there talked louder than these people could. I don't want to tell you any more. It is one dirt spot in the history of Germany which will never be washed off.[177]

Other friends from Gross Breesen and Hyde Farmlands came face to face with the tragedy of the Holocaust. They wrote their reactions in the *Circular Letters*, initially addressed to Bondy. Ernst Cramer, Bondy's assistant, returned to Buchenwald, the very same concentration camp he had been imprisoned in seven years earlier. As the open jeep bounced over potholes and craters, he sat pensively. The memories of the Krystallnacht pogrom on Gross Breesen occupied his mind, and in his haunted imagination, he traced the train ride to Buchenwald. He heard the screams and could feel the sharp stinging of the Nazi blows to his head. He could hear the

Töpper, in despair, witnessed the burials of the forced-labor prisoners at Wobbelin concentration camp. *Courtesy of the Angress family collection.*

snarling of German shepherds and the yelling of the SS guards. Then the jeep squealed to a stop.

> *We were right in front of the camp, on a road through which I had often been hounded. The first prisoners approached us, many of them stumbling. At the main gate, where the American soldiers were having some difficulty pushing back the masses of prisoners, a lieutenant greeted us...What we saw on that short path between the gate and the barracks made everything I went through in autumn 1938 shrink into meaninglessness.*
>
> *Figures marked by death came toward us. Some collapsed from the effort to speak. Others lay on the ground, their joints dislocated. When Henry tried to give some of these poor people something to eat, the lieutenant stopped him, saying: "If that man takes one bite of that rich food, he's a goner."*
>
> *Emaciated corpses were piled up like firewood. Others lay in scattered corners, seemingly unnoticed. People wearing rags, nothing but skin and bones, tried to speak to us. Some died right in front of us. The stench of corpses mixed with the smell of antiseptic lime.*

It was appalling. The thought that conditions must have been far worse in Auschwitz and other death camps was practically unbearable.[178]

One of the liberated prisoners at Buchenwald was a young, emaciated teenager. He could not avoid the poisoning effect of eating too much, and he became deathly sick, barely holding onto life for two weeks in the hospital. One day he got out of bed to see himself in a mirror. He had not seen himself ever since he was deported to Auschwitz and then marched to Buchenwald. He wrote later, "From the depth of the mirror, a corpse gazed back at me. The look in his eyes, as they stared into mine, has never left me."[179] That young survivor was Elie Wiesel, the future Nobel Prize winner and recipient of the Congressional Gold Medal who became the conscience and literary voice of the Holocaust.

Töpper's friend Ernst Cramer witnessed the liberation of Buchenwald. Elie Wiesel is pictured in the middle row, seventh from the left, next to the vertical post. *Courtesy USHMM 74607.*

Finding His Family

Soon after the end of the war was declared, Tom requested that he be allowed to return to Amsterdam to hunt for his family. General Gavin approved his request. Seeing so much devastation, dislocation and inhumanity, Tom feared the worst, but his hope defied the odds. Was it possible that his family had survived the war and Nazi occupation?

It was Mother's Day in May 1945. Tom started his search by returning to the house where he left his family on his journey to Hyde Farmlands almost six years before. An elderly man answered the door and, seeing he was an American soldier, asked, "Are you Werner Angress?" Those words, his name uttered by a stranger, startled Tom to the point of knocking the wind out of him. He was shocked. He did not know that his mother had advised the man that if her son ever came to look for her, she lived just a few doors away. Before Tom could answer, his mother appeared as if in a mirage.

On Mother's Day 1945, Tom Angress was reunited with his mother and two brothers in Amsterdam. His father had been murdered in Auschwitz. *Courtesy of the Angress family collection.*

She was alive, though emaciated; she weighed only ninety pounds. Such joy. She could not control her delirious crying for hours. Out of the shadows, Tom's two brothers joined the reunion. They all had survived by hiding with the help of the Dutch underground. His father had perished in Auschwitz.

The war was over. The agony of separation and never knowing if his family survived began to fade, but it would always be part of him. Tom felt he had lived through a storm, but in the end, he witnessed a miracle. Soon, the Angress family would start a new life in America.

Chapter 36

EVA, THE WAR YEARS

After Hyde Farmlands closed, Eva was uprooted once again, and she began a new chapter in her life. She never hesitated. She never stopped to wonder how she would manage to start all over again in a new place. She just did it. Along with several others from Hyde Farmlands, she worked as a counselor at Carson College Orphanage, near Philadelphia. There, she assisted the professional staff by interacting with the girls. After her stay at the orphanage, she moved to Detroit, Michigan. Family friends of her parents, the Sterbas, both psychiatrists, created a new home for her. They were refugees themselves, emigrating from Austria when Nazi Germany invaded in the 1938 Anschluss. Dr. Sterba, an associate of Sigmund Freud, was not a Jew, but he refused to collaborate with the Nazis. Eva's father knew him through his friendship with Freud. Their warm welcome of Eva softened the blow of starting over in a new place. Dr. Sterba was affiliated with Wayne State University in Detroit, so he encouraged Eva to enroll there to take courses to fill in the gaps in her high school education before she could apply to college. She completed those classes in May 1942. There was no question as to what her future profession was going to be. In Germany, she always dreamed of becoming a doctor, so her decision to study nursing was totally predictable. First, she had to contact St. Paul's Girls' School to procure her academic records. A letter of recommendation from her headmistress, Miss Strudwick, brought back so many memories, now five years later. Some were satisfying, especially with the buffer of time, and others were vividly tinged with the extreme pain of loneliness and anxiety. In a letter of recommendation from Dr. Curt Bondy, dated August 11, 1941, he stated, "I never saw a girl doing such a lot of work with so much enjoyment and helping the others so well. She has an especially good character, is absolutely truthful and reliable and has a strong social feeling." With great excitement, Eva was accepted to the Harper Hospital School of Nursing, a three-year registered nurse program that promised to be grueling.

Nurse Eva

Eva loved everything that was involved with nursing. Her passion to help patients in every way was immediately recognized by her teachers, supervisors, patients and fellow classmates. She felt perfectly comfortable on the floors interacting with the patients, and she excelled in the academics. The integration of classes and hands-on experiences in the hospital was the perfect balance. She was always very studious, but she could become impatient when there was no immediate application of what she learned. Nursing education was different. Even though the hours were terribly long—sometimes she would not sleep for thirty hours straight—she was always upbeat. She wrote in a letter, "My work in the hospital gives me great satisfaction and I feel very much at home with it. My head nurse and superiors are very much pleased with me and somehow that makes me very proud. I have been assigned a couple of very sick patients lately and it gives me confidence that I have no trouble in handling them, no matter how sick they are."[180]

Eva was accepted quickly by the other students; after all, she was now a young adult and not a fifteen-year-old transplant. But, no matter, she felt different from the others. She was a bit older than most, spoke with a mild German accent and had lived in places and experienced humiliation that the others could not even imagine. She was a German Jewish refugee whose memories could not be shared or truly understood. She confided in a letter:

> *At first, it disturbed me a little that I was really quite different from the girls, but now it does not matter anymore. I have found myself. I know what I want and nothing else matters. But there is always that last missing link in establishing a full contact with the girls. They do not realize it, and to them I am just one of the gang, and that is good. They come to me with their troubles and I try to help them. Sometimes I wonder why it is that people always seem to come to me with their troubles. It was like that in Hyde Farmlands, it was like that at the orphanage in Pennsylvania, and it is again like that here in the Nursing School. It happens to me when riding in a bus or train; people start talking, tell me their whole life history and troubles. And I often wonder why?*[181]

Eva possessed that unique quality that only sensitive listeners have: attentiveness. Her dark eyes focused with intent, and they communicated an accepting empathy. No wonder people sought her out for advice.

One weekend, several of her classmates and Eva drove north two hundred miles to a wilderness cabin owned by the family of a fellow student. Once they arrived, Eva sprang into action. To the astonishment of her friends, she started a fire

"Nurse Eva" at the historic Harper Hospital School of Nursing, Detroit, Michigan. *Courtesy of the Eva Loew collection.*

217

even with wet wood. It felt wonderful to split the logs, just as she did at Hyde Farmlands to feed the wood stove and the furnace. The memories of her past never dimmed.

Farmer Eva

Eva was very fortunate to have a friend from Gross Breesen living in Michigan. Heinz Loeser and his wife, Anne, owned a farm near Decatur, two hundred miles west of Detroit. Eva described the town as "tiny…about the size of Crewe [Virginia] with farms and orchards all around it." Whenever she could, Eva escaped the city and visited the farm on the weekends. She was always welcomed, and the minute she arrived, she changed into her overalls. She wrote:

> *I helped Heinz out at the barn with some repair jobs and then picked tomatoes. You should have seen my hands, just as black as can be and that was not a sun tan either…After supper, I helped with the chores, gave the hogs water and taught a little bull calf how to drink out of a bucket. Also, I milked one of the two cows…it's a year since I have milked a cow…but I can still milk so that there is lots of foam on top of the milk in the bucket.*[182]

Eva had a special place in her heart for dairy cows. It started at Gross Breesen and expanded with her responsibilities at Hyde Farmlands. She was delighted to milk a cow again, for she loved "the feeling of leaning her head against the cow's flank and smell[ing] that smell so full of the outdoors, the pasture and the sunshine."[183] A deep affection for farming ran through her veins, and she loved the quiet beauty of the rural setting. At times, she had a desperate longing for the country, "for some pine tree to sit under and smell, for the early mornings full of dew and for the evenings and nights free from any city noises. [She] wanted to see a field of wheat golden in the sunshine and…watch the wind blow over it and make waves in it…to smell the freshly cut and dried hay and a field of red clover in bloom…to lie down and just look up at the sky through the tree tops."[184] For Eva, experiencing the beauty of nature was religious, bringing tears to her eyes; she knew it was the "greatest joy."

Nurse Cadet "Jakie"

She juggled studies with intensely long shifts of nursing patients. While she was in training, she was inducted into the U.S. Cadet Nurse Corps. This meant that she pledged to stay in essential nursing for the duration of the war. She would wear a military uniform, receive twenty dollars a month and agree to be sent to any military hospital (except overseas) for the last six months of her training. In January 1945, she was deployed to Percy Jones Army Hospital in Battlecreek, Michigan, where she would care for returning wounded military. She was the first foreign-born army nurse cadet in the nation, and she became the poster nurse for cadet recruitment. At Percy, Eva became part of regular army life. She slept in barracks, ate in the mess hall, learned military protocol, drilled with a gas mask and practiced marching drills as part of her basic training. In short, nurse cadets were treated like regular army nurses and had almost the same authority and privileges. She received one half day per week and one full day a month to catch up on her rest, but that did not relieve her long shifts. She was continually exhausted.

Just before she moved to Percy, she was joyously and proudly granted U.S. citizenship on December 14, 1944. As she wrote in a letter, "Tomorrow will be a big day for me. I finally got a letter telling me to come for my final hearing and by the time you get this letter, I will be a citizen of this country!!! Congratulations are in order now…I am going to wear my uniform when I go down there and am very excited about it already."[185]

For Eva, the only way she could get into the fight to defeat the Nazis was to be an army nurse. As the battles raged in Europe, severely wounded soldiers were transported back to the States for hospitalization and medical care. Tragically, many of the wounded soldiers were amputees. Eva worked in the post-amputation ward, where she

Eva in her army nurse cadet uniform at Percy Jones Army Hospital, Battle Creek, Michigan. *Courtesy of the Eva Loew collection.*

dressed the stumps of these wounded soldiers, and as she did, the haunting question always arose: Would the next B-17 medical transport plane carry someone she knew and loved? Every time a new patient arrived, she prayed that he would not be one of her friends from Gross Breesen or Hyde Farmlands. Every time she entered the ICU, she paused and held her breath.

Eva was a skilled nurse, but it was her personality that captured the hearts of the wounded patients. She was so approachable, one to kid and tease. The soldiers nicknamed her "Jake" or "Jakie," a shortened form of her last name, Jacobsohn. They were comfortable with her and entrusted her with their care. She gained the reputation of being the best changer of dressings on their amputated limbs. She masked her true feelings well. She wrote:

> *You know people say that after a while you get used to things like seeing people suffer or the amputations, etc. I don't see how anybody could get used to that, anybody that has a heart and not a piece of stone instead. Every time again, when I see a 19 year old or even younger, one with both the legs or arms off, it hits me all over again…the boys, so many of them, really are in bad pain and they take it so well…they kid around regardless of how they feel and thank you for the least little bit you do for them.* [186]

Eva would do anything to ease the pain of her soldiers:

> *Yesterday afternoon there was a period with not very much to do,*
> *so I went around chatting a little with the bed-patients, the ones*
> *that are not allowed to get up and around at all. One of them had*
> *just gotten a big harmonica and they asked me to play. Of course,*
> *I had never played on one, but it was only a few minutes before*
> *I picked out a number of tunes and then we really went to town.*
> *The boys liked it and tried to think of songs for me to play so I*
> *would not stop, and I had to make the rounds on the ward and*
> *play a few songs in each section. We really had a lot of fun for*
> *a while. You should have seen it. They wiggled their toes in their*
> *casts to beat out the rhythm and really had a big time.*[187]

Eva could never stop worrying about "her Boys" who were in the midst of battle. One of her boys was particularly dear. She had fallen in love with Ernst Loew (Loewensberg), a Bondy assistant at Gross Breesen, who was stationed in England and later in Germany. She and Ernst had worked side by side in the early days of Hyde Farmlands. There, they recognized the qualities in each other that they dearly admired. Both were refugees, both had limitless confidence in their ability to create a farm and both planned their future lives together as farmers.

In addition to her nursing activities, Eva sought out ways to assist the war effort. Even though she could not afford it, she regularly purchased war bonds, and she donated blood, which, as a nurse, she was not supposed to do. She even found time to knit Ernst a warm wool sweater because she knew "it gets darn cold over there."[188] But above all, she wrote countless letters from "home." In reality, Eva was the only family some of the men had. Among others, she wrote to Töpper, and to Ernst alone, she wrote 206 letters between 1942 and 1945. Even after long, exhausting hours in the hospital, every night, she wrote to her friends overseas and sent them care packages. She was the lifeline anchor for so many. Tom sent her his Purple Heart medal for safekeeping, for in his mind, if Eva were safe, he would be safe also.

Eva was the symbol of hope. In the middle of the Michigan winter, she planted narcissus bulbs in her room and nurtured their early blooming as she listened to the music of Mozart, "her way of cracking the ice of fear."[189] Tellingly, she always spelled Spring with a capital letter.

The letters, "V-mail," written to Ernst revealed what Eva held dear in her heart and mind. Once, she hiked alone to the top of a high hill. She recounted:

> *I just wanted to shout with joy when I had climbed to the top of the biggest one and could see the blue lakes below and the woods and fields around the lakes. And I could not help but think that this is part of all the things that we are fighting for…These few moments of happiness are so rare and precious in our time that is so full of hatred, insecurity and nastiness. I am so grateful for…such places give one strength and courage to go on and face the world.*[190]

Eva could not ignore a nagging feeling that she could not quite put her finger on. It was like having a sliver under the surface of her skin. It could not be seen, and tweezers could not grab it. But she knew it was there. It was her past. She could never escape it. On November 11, 1942, she wrote to Ernst:

> *I can't help but think of those November days only four years ago, those fateful terrible days.* [Krystallnacht, November 9–10, 1938]*…I promise to myself and to the people who cannot fight anymore, that I shall do anything that is in my power, anything to help prevent those things from happening again. I feel that I owe it to all who are no longer with us.*[191]

In another letter, she acknowledged their stunted youth:

> *We, both of us, have spent so much of our lives in abnormal circumstances and environments, have missed so much that ordinary people have. Just someday, I would like to be in normal surroundings, living a normal life and bringing up my kids that way too, so they won't have to miss all the things we had to miss, so they will have a place where they belong and grow up the way they should, and not the way we did.*[192]

She missed Ernst dreadfully, but she looked to the future when the two could farm and raise a family in peace. She knew herself well: "I get such joy out of seeing things grow and develop and I guess that's one of the reasons why I lost my heart to farming. And it's something that is close to nursing, too, because that profession is a constructive one, and in cases where that is impossible, it is at least a supportive one."[193]

Chapter 37

BONDY AND THALHIMER, THE WAR YEARS

When the war broke out, Bondy volunteered for the draft, but he was too old. The only way he could get into the fight to defeat Nazi Germany was to support the hearts and minds of his Gross Breesen students. He knew the brutality of war from his own experience in World War I, and he worried that combat could destroy a person, physically and emotionally. He had faith that his "boys" would emerge stronger than before. He reasoned that the lives of refugees and soldiers in battle were similar: "[That if people] endure great hardship and suffer much misfortune, [they] either become purposeless and perish or actually grow, because of all the difficulties, [people can] become deeper and emerge as greater and stronger personalities from these times."[194]

He hoped that his personal letters would motivate his students toward greater awareness, a greater sense of controlling the moment, no matter how chaotic it may have been. Bondy believed that misfortune was like a treatment, a chemotherapy of the spirit. He knew the power of pain. It would either cure or kill, but unlike the fight against a physical disease, one could hopefully exert enough spiritual will to survive.

Even during periods of combat, Hyde Farmlanders wrote letters to Bondy, who, in turn, published them in the continual dissemination of the *Circular Letters*. They revealed the serious thoughts of the soldiers as they pushed deeper toward Germany. Even when battles were raging, their letters contained questions about what they would do after the war was over. Bondy thought that these concerns about the future were hopeful signs, but he acknowledged that the Hyde Farmlanders faced complications once they returned to the United States: they did not have

This cover of a *Circular Letters* installment captured the transition from farming to military service in World War II. *Courtesy of the* Circular Letters.

homes, families or professions to come back to. He answered their predicament positively:

> *When the time comes that we can expect you back, you can be sure that we will organize things in a way that all of you will find a home and people who will be very glad to have you with them, and where you would really like to go. So I think the first problem, namely where you will go after your discharge can be easily and satisfactorily solved. To be sure about this will give you a feeling of security.*[195]

He tried to help the soldiers focus on matters that went beyond day-to-day survival. He recommended that each think about what he wanted to do in the future and asked how each could possibly obtain training for that profession or vocation while still in the army.

Bondy, too, looked to the future. He continued his teaching at the Richmond Professional Institute, where he introduced a new course that trained counselors who would be advising returning servicemen/women in their endeavors to map out a new life. As early as 1942–43, he and social psychologist Bruno Bettelheim wrote about concentration camp life in an article that was published in the *Journal of Abnormal and Social Psychology*. He realized that such insights would someday be crucial in rehabilitating both inmates and jailers. At the time, Bondy never imagined that the brutality he experienced in Buchenwald in 1938 would be dwarfed when compared to the crematoriums of the Holocaust.

THALHIMER

William B. Thalhimer also corresponded with Hyde Farmlanders during the war. Even though he was weakened by his heart condition, he threw himself into the war effort by heading war bond campaigns. He continued to be involved in refugee resettlement matters, though immigration halted after the war began. He realized that for the time being, he had done all he could. His attention shifted to activities that supported the soldiers. One of his most favorite was the staging of block parties in the parking lot of Thalhimer's Department Store for soldiers stationed near Richmond. Here, soldiers from the area came to relax and socialize with volunteers. These successful weekly parties became famous throughout the region.

After the war, Bondy and Thalhimer agreed that military service achieved four key objectives for the students of Hyde Farmlands: one, everyone learned English very well; two, all were Americanized; three, all became American citizens; and four, many benefited from the GI Bill with its educational opportunities.

In the fall of 1945, Töpper returned to Thalhimer's store office with a few Hyde Farmlanders, all veterans of the European campaign. There, he embraced Thalhimer and Bondy. His thoughts returned to the first time he met Thalhimer almost six years before. Thalhimer beamed with pride as he introduced Tom to the store employees. Morton Thalhimer, William's cousin, praised him and pointed to his medals as he proclaimed, "When this boy came to this country, he was just a little refugee, and look at him now!"[196]

The letters that Eva and Bondy sent to the Hyde Farmland soldiers anchored them to the enduring values of Gross Breesen: those of hope, courage and resiliency. Bondy closed his letters with words that would resonate throughout the lives of the students and even their offspring: "Remain Gross Breeseners." He knew that the students had inhabited Gross Breesen, the place, but he always hoped that Gross Breesen would inhabit the students, and it did.

Chapter 38

"THEY WHO SOW IN TEARS"

They who sow in tears
Shall reap with songs of joy.
Though he goes along weeping,
Carrying the seed-bag,
He shall come back with songs of joy,
Carrying his sheaves.
—Psalm 126:5–6

Tom and Eva sowed their youth with tears, but they were the fortunate ones because they were nurtured by adults who committed themselves to their safety and welfare. When their adolescence was stolen from them by the Nazis, Curt Bondy's Gross Breesen taught them life lessons that fortified them throughout their lifetimes. William B. Thalhimer literally rescued them by fighting for their visas and providing them with a home in Virginia. As the war was coming to an end, the horrors of the Holocaust became known to a traumatized world. Every Gross Breesener who escaped and was scattered all over the world gave thanks for being alive. The Jews living in the towns surrounding Gross Breesen were some of the first to be transported to Auschwitz.

With the war over, Tom and Eva launched themselves into their new lives. Tom enrolled under the GI Bill at Wesleyan University in Connecticut and graduated magna cum laude in 1949. He then earned his PhD in history and became a very popular university professor of European and German history. He was the recipient of the SUNY Chancellor's Award for Excellence in Teaching and the History Department Outstanding Professor Award at Stony Brook University. He wrote several books, some about his experiences in Nazi Germany as a teenager. After he retired, he never stopped teaching and writing; he returned to Germany to help young German students understand what it was like to grow up as a German Jew in the 1930s and learn the lessons of vile and tragic racism. He worked for the civil rights of minorities. When Tom looked back on his military experiences, he concluded that the army provided him with "a refuge, a home, and in a way, a family."[197]

Eva combined her love of farming and nursing throughout her entire life. She married a fellow Gross Breesener, Ernst Loew (Loewensberg), and together they created a successful dairy farm in eastern Connecticut. Their dairy farm was so exceptional that it became a teaching laboratory for university agricultural interns. Eva never lost her love for cows, and she even piped classical music into the barn for their enjoyment. Her six children were raised on the farm, and whenever they complained about the work, Eva would admonish them: "Where is your Gross Breesen spirit?" She lovingly confided that "in the morning, she delivered babies in the hospital, and in the afternoon, she delivered calves in the barn."[198] During his college years, Tom visited Eva and Ernst on their farm in Norwich, Connecticut, and as soon as he arrived, he changed into work clothes to earn his keep.

To this day, to honor Eva, the town of Hampton, Connecticut, awards the EVA Award to the most deserving volunteer who has contributed to the welfare of the town. "EVA" stands for "Extraordinary Valuable Asset."

In 1991, Eva returned to her home in Marienfelde, Germany, to witness the dedication of a street sign, a memorial to her father.

Dr. Curt Bondy returned to Germany to teach a new generation of psychology students who had never studied Freud and other Jewish

Left: Werner T. Angress, in retirement, returned to Germany to teach young Germans about Nazi racism and fight for the civil rights of minorities. *Courtesy of the Angress family collection.*

Below: The author visiting Eva and her daughter, Jacqueline Jacobsohn, at Eva's Connecticut dairy farm. *Courtesy of Marsha Gillette.*

thinkers. He once again became a popular and revered professor and was elected president of the German Psychological Association.

In 1954, William B. Thalhimer received the Richmond Jewish Community Council Award for Distinguished Service. His tireless work on behalf of refugees stood out: "But if nothing else had been accomplished by this all-important individual, except helping to save these victims of oppression from Hitler's Germany this would have been enough to place him in the annals of history. What he has done for suffering humanity at home and abroad."[199]

On April 21, 2013, exactly seventy-five years to the day after William B. Thalhimer took ownership of Hyde Farmlands, Hyde Park Farm was dedicated as a National and Virginia Historic Site. Thalhimer's descendants gathered to read the historic roadside marker and celebrate the story of rescue.

Gross Breeseners lived throughout the world, but they managed to gather for reunions. They never lost their Gross Breesen spirit, but they never could totally overcome the haunting reality that they left families behind, never to see them again.

Both Tom Angress and Eva Loew were "extraordinary valuable assets." They sowed their youth with tears, but they carried seeds of joy and planted them throughout their lifetimes. Their arms never tired carrying the sheaves of the fullness of life.

NOTES

Abbreviations

ED: Eva Jacobsohn's unpublished diary
EL: Eva Jacobsohn's wartime unpublished letters
CL: Circular Letters

Chapter 1

1. Angress, *Witness to the Storm*, 76.
2. Ibid., 75.
3. Ibid., 70.
4. Ibid., 73.
5. Ibid., 63.
6. Ibid., 79.
7. Ibid., 81.
8. Strom, *Facing History and Ourselves*, 214.
9. Hughes and Mann, *Inside Hitler's Germany*, 52.

Chapter 3

10. *CL*, 19.

Chapter 4

11. Angress, *Witness to the Storm*, 134.

Chapter 5

12. *CL*, 27.
13. Angress, *...immer etwas abseits*, 144.
14. *CL*, 27.
15. Angress, *Between Fear and Hope*, 50.
16. Ibid., 52.
17. *CL*, 46.
18. Angress, *Between Fear and Hope*, 52.
19. Angress, *Witness to the Storm*, 146.
20. *CL*, 28–29.
21. Angress, *Between Fear and Hope*, 54.
22. Angress, *Witness to the Storm*, 141–42.

Chapter 6

23. EL, June 1, 1944.
24. Ibid., June 13, 1944.
25. Conversation with Eva Loew.
26. Ibid.
27. *American Jewish Committee Report*, 1933, 36.
28. ED, July 12, 1936.

Chapter 7

29. Eva Jacobsohn wrote a daily diary at St. Paul's Girls' School.
30. Bailes, *Once a Paulina*, 51.
31. ED, October 5, 1936.
32. Ibid., July 12, 1936.
33. Bailes, *Once a Paulina*, 34.
34. ED, July 12, 1936.

Chapter 8

35. Ibid., July 22, 1936.
36. Ibid., July 25, 1936.
37. Ibid., July 30, 1936.
38. Ibid.
39. Ibid., August 10, 1936.

Chapter 9

40. Ibid., September 21, 1936.
41. Ibid., September 22, 1936.

42. Ibid., September 13, 1936.
43. Ibid., September 22, 1936.
44. Ibid., October 21, 1936.
45. Ibid., September 22, 1936.
46. Ibid.
47. Ibid., September 30, 1936.
48. Ibid.
49. Ibid., October 4, 1936.
50. Ibid., October 14, 1936.
51. Ibid., October 11, 1936.
52. Ibid., October 16, 1936.
53. Ibid., October 23, 1936.

Chapter 10

54. Ibid., November 22, 1936.
55. Ibid., November 8, 1936.
56. Ibid.
57. Ibid., December 10, 1936.
58. Ibid., April 29, 1937.
59. Ibid., May 8, 1937.
60. Ibid., May 12, 1937.
61. Ibid.

Chapter 11

62. Ibid., August 18, 1937.
63. *CL*, 46.
64. ED, June 24, 1937.
65. Ibid., July 19, 1937.

Chapter 12

66. Ibid., October 4, 1937.
67. Interview with Jacqueline Jacobsohn, December 29, 2014.
68. *CL*, 45.
69. ED, September 7, 1938.
70. *CL*, 46.

Chapter 13

71. Ibid.
72. Ibid., "Bondy Report," 1937, 99.

73. Angress, *Between Fear and Hope*, 49.
74. *CL*, 65.
75. Angress, *Witness to the Storm*, 153.
76. *CL*, 46.
77. Angress, *Witness to the Storm*, 155.

Chapter 14
78. Angress, *Between Fear and Hope*, 54–55.

Chapter 15
79. Angress, *Witness to the Storm*, 147–48.

Chapter 16
80. Ibid., 148.
81. Ibid., 150–52.

Chapter 17
82. Ibid., 138–39.
83. *CL*, 392.
84. Angress, *Witness to the Storm*, 140–41.

Chapter 18
85. *CL*, 121.
86. ED, September 7, 1938.
87. *CL*, 129–30.
88. Ibid.
89. Ibid., 155.

Chapter 19
90. Angress, *Witness to the Storm*, 156.
91. Ibid., 157.
92. Ibid.
93. Ibid., 159.

Chapter 20
94. Interview with Jacqueline Jacobsohn.
95. ED, October 13, 1938.
96. Ibid.

Chapter 21

97. Interview with Eva Loew, February 1, 2012.
98. ED, September 7, 1938.
99. Ibid., October 13, 1938.
100. Ibid.
101. Ibid.
102. Ibid.
103. Ibid.
104. Ibid., December 28, 1938.
105. Ibid.
106. Ibid.
107. Ibid.
108. Ibid., February 8, 1939.

Chapter 22

109. Gillette, *Virginia Plan*, 84.
110. *CL*, 318.
111. Ibid., 259.
112. Ibid., 260.
113. Ibid.
114. ED, April 10, 1939.
115. Eanes, *Memories of Virginia Conservation Corps Camps.*
116. Gillette, *Virginia Plan*, 113.

Chapter 23

117. Angress, *Witness to the Storm*, 181.
118. Ibid., 182.
119. Angress, *Between Fear and Hope*, 231.

Chapter 24

120. Cohn, *No Justice in Germany*, 181.
121. Ibid., 189.
122. Gilbert, *Krystallnacht*, 79.
123. Ibid., 48.
124. Ibid., 29.
125. Esther Adler, August 2007.
126. NA, RG 59, 862.40, 6/1813, M 1284, Roll 22, November 10, 1938.
127. Gilbert, *Krystallnacht*, 29.

128. Ibid.

129. *CL*, 155.

130. Ibid., 1205.

131. Angress, *Between Fear and Hope*, 166.

CHAPTER 25

132. E. Cramer, essay, *CL*, 1572.

133. Curt Bondy, "Problems of Internment Camps," *CL*, 245.

134. Harvey Newton, *Buchenwald Reminiscences, 1944, CL*, 1205.

135. Curt Bondy, "Testament," *CL*, 426.

136. Ibid.

137. Ibid., 247.

CHAPTER 26

138. Angress, *Witness to the Storm*, 187.

139. Ibid., 188.

140. Ibid.

141. See Gillette, *Virginia Plan*, chapter 9.

CHAPTER 27

142. Angress, *Between Fear and Hope*, 103.

143. Ibid.

144. NA, Roll 22, December 10, 1938.

145. Angress, *Witness to the Storm*, 192.

146. Angress, *Between Fear and Hope*, 112.

CHAPTER 28

147. NA, RG 811.11184, Box 231, H.F., May 22, 1939.

148. Ibid.

CHAPTER 29

149. *CL*, 245.

150. Angress, *Between Fear and Hope*, 119.

151. Ibid., 119–20.

CHAPTER 30

152. Angress, *Witness to the Storm*, 200.

153. Ibid.

154. Ibid., 203.
155. Ibid., 207.

Chapter 31

156. Ibid., 211.
157. Gillette, *Virginia Plan*, 140.
158. Angress, *...immer etwas abseits*, 279–80.

Chapter 32

159. Gillette, *Virginia Plan*, see chapter 15.

Chapter 33

160. Angress, unpublished Hyde Farmlands diary, May 20, 1940.
161. Ibid.
162. *CL*, 400.

Chapter 34

163. Angress, HF diary, February 14, 1941.
164. *CL*, 470–71.
165. Ibid., 428.
166. Ibid., 463.
167. Ibid., 442.
168. Angress, *Witness to the Storm*, 226.

Chapter 35

169. Ibid., 211.
170. Ibid., 232–33.
171. Ibid., 243.
172. Ibid., 277.
173. Ibid., 273.
174. Ibid., 293.
175. Ibid., 303.
176. Ibid., 314.
177. *Times-Dispatch*, June 4, 1945.
178. *CL*, 1572–73.
179. Wiesel, *Night*, 109.

Chapter 36

180. EL, October 3, 1942.
181. Ibid.
182. Ibid., August 21, 1944.
183. Ibid., August 30, 1942.
184. Ibid., July 29, 1944.
185. Ibid., December 13, 1944.
186. Ibid., February 26, 1945.
187. Ibid., February 6, 1945.
188. Ibid., September 22, 1944.
189. Jacqueline Jacobsohn's description in conversation.
190. EL, August 30, 1942.
191. Ibid., November 11, 1942.
192. Ibid., May 27, 1945.
193. Ibid., January 2, 1945.

Chapter 37

194. *CL*, 470–74.
195. Ibid., 558.
196. EL, October 28, 1945.

Chapter 38

197. Angress, *Witness to the Storm*, 328.
198. EL, January 2, 1945.
199. Samuel Troy, RJCC Award Banquet, 1954.

BIBLIOGRAPHY

BOOKS

Altman, Linda Jacobs. *Hitler's Rise to Power and the Holocaust*. Berkeley Heights, NJ: Enslow Publishers, 2003.

——. *The Jewish Victims of the Holocaust*. Berkeley Heights, NJ: Enslow Publishers, 2003.

Angress, Werner T. *Between Fear and Hope*. New York: Columbia University Press, 1988.

——. *...immer etwas abseits, Jugenderinnerungen eines judischen Berliners 1920–1945*. Berlin: Edition Hentich, 2005.

——. Personal diary (unpublished), 1938–41.

——. *Witness to the Storm*. Durham, NC: printed by CreateSpace, 2012.

Ascher, Abraham. *A Community Under Siege: The Jews of Breslau Under Nazism*. Stanford, CA: Stanford University Press, 2012.

Bailes, Howard. *Once a Paulina: A History of St. Paul's Girls' School*. London: James and James, 2000.

Baker, Leonard. *Days of Sorrow and Pain: Leo Baeck and the Berlin Jews*. New York: Macmillan Publishing Co., Inc., 1978.

Bartoletti, Susan Campbell. *Hitler's Youth: Growing Up in Hitler's Shadow*. New York: Scholastic Inc., 2005.

Bauer, Yehuda. *A History of the Holocaust*. Danbury, CT: Franklin Watts, 2001.

BIBLIOGRAPHY

————. *Rethinking the Holocaust*. New Haven, CT: Yale University Press, 2001.

Bessel, Richard. *Life in the Third Reich*. Oxford, UK: Oxford, 2001.

Cohn, Willy. *No Justice in Germany*. Stanford, CA: Stanford University Press, 2012.

Covington, Julian, and Edwina Covington. *Tobacco Rows in Prince Edward County*. Appomattox, VA: Village Print Shop, 2006.

Crowe, David M. *The Holocaust: Roots, History, and Aftermath*. Boulder, CO: Westview Press, 2008.

Eanes, Greg. *Memories of Virginia Conservation Corps Camps*. Crewe, VA: E&H Printing, 1999.

Echoes and Reflections: Teacher's Resource Guide. New York: Anti-Defamation League, 2014.

Evans, Richard J. *The Coming of the Third Reich*. New York: Penguin Books, 2005.

Frankl, Viktor E. *Man's Search for Meaning*. New York: Simon & Schuster, 1984.

Friedlander, Saul. *Nazi Germany and the Jews*. Vol. 1, *The Years of Persecution, 1933–1939*. London: Phoenix Giant, 1998.

Gilbert, Martin. *Krystallnacht: Prelude to Destruction*. London: Harper Press, 2006.

Gillette, Robert H. *The Virginia Plan: William B. Thalhimer and a Rescue from Nazi Germany*. Charleston, SC: The History Press, 2011.

Greenfeld, Howard. *The Hidden Children*. New York: Ticknor and Fields, 1993.

Hughes, Matthew, and Chris Mann. *Inside Hitler's Germany*. New York: MJF Books, 2000.

Luckert, Steven, and Susan Bachrach. *State of Deception: The Power of Nazi Propaganda*. Washington, D.C.: United States Holocaust Memorial Museum, 2011.

Meyer, Michael A., ed. *German-Jewish History in Modern Times*. New York: Columbia University Press, 1998.

Mowrer, Edgar A. *Germany Puts the Clock Back*. New York: William Morrow and Company, 1933.

Niewyk, Donald L. *The Jews in Weimar Germany*. New Brunswick: Transaction Publishers, 2001.

Soumerai, Eve Nussbaum, and Carol D. Schulz. *Daily Life During the Holocaust*. Westport, CT: Greenwood Press, 1998.

BIBLIOGRAPHY

————. *Human Rights: The Struggle for Freedom, Dignity and Equality.* CT: State Board of Education, 1998.

————. *A Voice from the Holocaust.* Westport, CT: Greenwood Press, 2003.

Strom, Margot Stern. *Facing History and Ourselves: Holocaust and Human Behavior.* Brookline, MA: Facing History and Ourselves, 1994.

Wiesel, Elie. *Night.* New York: Bantam Books, 1960.

Wood, Angela Gluck. *Holocaust.* New York: DK Publishing, 2007.

Wyman, David S. *The Abandonment of the Jews.* New York: New Press, 1998.

————. *Paper Walls: America and the Refugee Crisis, 1938–1941.* New York: Pantheon Books, 1985.

Zucker, Bat Ami. *In Search of Refuge: Jews and US Consuls in Nazi Germany 1933–1941.* Parkes-Wiener Series on Jewish Studies. Portland, OR: Valentine, 2001.

For an extensive bibliography of 1930s Germany and the Jews, refer to the bibliography in *The Virginia Plan: William B. Thalhimer and a Rescue from Nazi Germany* by Robert H. Gillette (The History Press, 2011).

PERIODICALS AND JOURNALS

Boas, Jacob. "German-Jewish Internal Politics Under Hitler, 1933–1938." *Leo Baeck Institute Year Book* 29 (1984): 3–25.

Breitman, Richard, Alan M. Kraut and Thomas Imhoof. "The State Department, the Labor Department, and German Jewish Immigration, 1930–1940." *Journal of American Ethnic History* 3, no. 2 (Spring 1984).

Loewenberg, Peter. "Krystallnacht as a Public Degradation Ritual." *Leo Baeck Institute Year Book* (1987): 309–23.

Schatzker, Chaim. "The Jewish Youth Movement in Germany in the Holocaust Period: Youth in Confrontation with a New Reality." *Leo Baeck Institute Year Book* (1987): 157–81.

————. "Martin Buber's Influence on the Jewish Youth Movement in Germany." *Leo Baeck Institute Year Book* 19 (1974): 77–95.

Schneiderman, Harry, ed. *American Jewish Committee Year Book* (October 1, 1932–September 21, 1941): 34–42. Jewish Publication Society, Philadelphia.

BIBLIOGRAPHY

Shafir, Shlomo. "American Diplomats in Berlin 1933–39 and Their Attitude to the Nazi Persecution of the Jews." *Yad Vashem Studies on the European Jewish Catastrophe and Resistance* 9 (n.d.): 71–104. Jerusalem.

Stahl, Rudoph. "Vocational Retraining of Jews in Nazi Germany 1933–1938." *Jewish Social Studies* 1, no. 2 (April 1939): 169–94.

Tolischus, Otto D. "Trouble-Shooter in Berlin." *New York Times Magazine*, July 23, 1039.

Zucker, Bat-Ami. "Francis Perkins and the German-Jewish Refugees, 1933–1940." *Journal of American Jewish Historical Society* 89, no. 1 (March 2001): 35–59.

Archival Collections

Several archival collections provided primary materials. The *Circular Letters*, the *Rundbriefe*, is a massive collection of letters, news reports, documents, personal essays and reunion reports all related to the students of Gross Breesen. This gigantic collection, begun in 1936 and continuing today, owes its existence to the enormous efforts of Herbert P. Cohn (Herko), who immigrated to Australia in the late 1930s with a Gross Breesen contingent. The *Circular Letters* is digitized matter available on the Internet at http://grossbreesensilesia.com.

Eva Jacobsohn Loew's extensive private diaries and archives cover her stay at St. Paul's Girls' School in England, her stay at Gross Breesen and her time in Cuba. Her letters to Ernst Loew include the war years when she was attending nursing school and as an army cadet nurse.

Werner Angress, in addition to *Between Hope and Fear* and *Witness to the Storm*, shared his Hyde Farmlands private diary.

In addition to written materials, the author made extensive notes from his interviews and conversations with Eva and Werner.

Werner T. Angress. Private Hyde Farmlands diary.

Circular Letters.

Eva Jacobsohn Loew. Private diary at Gross Breesen, Germany.

———. Private England diary.

———. Private work diary at Hyde Farmlands, Virginia.

———. Private World War II letters.

National Archives: State Department Records. Microfilm: RG 59, M1284.

BIBLIOGRAPHY

————. RG 59.

————. RG 59, Curt Bondy, 811.11184.

————. RG 59, Refugees, 811.11184.

————. RG 59, Stack 230, Compartment 23, Shelf 07, labeled NND775007, Box 231, 811.1185/231.

Richmond Times-Dispatch.

Thalhimer family archives. Richmond, Virginia.

Virginia Holocaust Museum Archives. Richmond, Virginia.

Photographic Collections

Angress family collection.

Abraham Ascher private collection.

Robert Gillette private collection.

Jerzy Kos private collection.

Eva Loew private collection.

Steven Strauss Gross Breesen Collection. Gross Breesen Project, www.grossbreesen.com.

Thalhimer family private collection.

United States Holocaust Memorial Museum Photographic Archives.

Virginia Holocaust Museum Archives.

Wratislaviae Amici doiny-slask Collection (Poland).

INDEX

A

Anschluss 146, 215
Arbiter 77
Ascher, Esther 14, 149, 150
Auschwitz 209, 212, 214, 228

B

bar mitzvah 35, 36
Barnes, Jackson, Wilkins,
        Jennings 205
Blaupunkts 60
Borchardt, Friedrich 112
Breslau, Germany 39, 43, 44, 88,
        118, 119, 121, 148, 149,
        151, 152, 154, 156, 164, 165
Bryan, John Stuart 195
Buchenwald Concentration Camp
        155, 156, 161, 162, 163,
        164, 165, 166, 170, 195,
        196, 210, 212, 226
Bund 26, 27, 28, 31, 43, 45, 46,
        52, 73, 77, 147, 170, 204
Burkeville, Virginia 17, 113, 131,
        132, 143, 168, 178, 195

Bute House 64, 66, 67, 69, 75,
        89, 94

C

Camp Ritchie 206
CCC (Civilian Conservation
        Corps) 142, 143, 187
Cohen, Leroy 167, 168
Cohn, Dr. Willy 148, 149
coronation 81, 82
Crewe, Virginia 186, 187, 204, 218
Cunningham, Janet (Bute House)
        64, 65, 68

D

D-Day 207, 208

E

Einstein, Albert 58, 131
Elk, Rudolf 162
EVA Award 229
Eva's passport 125, 126

INDEX

F

"Faterland" 26, 70
Franken, U.K. 135, 200

G

Gavin, Major General James M.
    207, 213
Geist, Consul General Raymond
    113, 114, 163, 164
Gerson, Martin 165
Gross Breesen Educational
    Agenda 42

H

Hanukkah 165
Harper Hospital School of
    Nursing 216, 217
Hindenburg dirigible 82
Hyde Farmlands 115, 116, 117,
    131, 132, 135, 142, 143,
    144, 146, 163, 173, 176,
    178, 179, 181, 188, 189,
    193, 194, 195, 196, 197,
    198, 200, 201, 203, 204,
    205, 210, 213, 215, 217,
    218, 220, 221, 227, 231
Hyde Park Farm 115, 231

I

"inferior race" 59

J

Juden 60, 125, 149
Jungfolk (Hitler Youth) 26

K

Kafka, Franz 96
Kiddush 58
King Edward VIII 81

klutz 45
Krystallnacht 148, 149, 151, 153,
    154, 161, 163, 165, 210, 222

L

Lanz Bulldog tractor 53, 54
lebenskunde ("life lessons") 96
Lessing's *Nathan the Wise* 98
Loeser, Anne and Heinz 218
Loewensberg, Joseph 176

M

Marienfelde, Germany 56, 71, 229
Matric exam 61, 74, 77, 84, 86

N

Nazi "Final Solution" 17, 150, 209
Nuremberg Laws 28, 38

O

ober 54, 92, 93, 139
Oder River 88, 107
116th Infantry Regiment, 29th
    Virginia National Guard
    Division 205, 208

P

Percy Jones Army Hospital 219, 220

R

Reich Youth Sports Badge 23
Rhohr family 39
Rundbriefe (*Circular Letters*) 170, 171,
    173, 210, 225, 244

S

Schloss (Gross Breesen "castle")
    44, 45, 47, 48, 52, 89, 92,
    96, 97, 119, 122, 129, 154

INDEX

Schwarzchild, Fritz 165
Shabbat (Sabbath) 36, 48, 58, 76,
       103, 165, 187
Southern States 140
Sterba, Dr. 215
St. Paul's Girls' School, England
       61, 63, 64, 65, 67, 74, 75,
       76, 80, 85, 86, 90, 152, 215
Strudwick, Ethel (headmistress of
       St. Paul's) 66, 81, 216

T

Thalhimer Department Store 112,
       176, 177, 227
Thalhimer, Morton 132, 198,
       199, 227
Thalhimer, William B. 112, 113,
       114, 115, 116, 132, 135,
       137, 140, 145, 152, 163,
       164, 166, 167, 168, 169,
       174, 176, 178, 184, 185,
       186, 193, 198, 200, 226,
       227, 228, 230, 231

V

van Tijn, Gertrude 162
Virginia Cooperative Service 139
Virginia Plan 113, 114, 122, 125,
       167, 178

W

Warren, Avra 163
Werkdorf Nieuwesluis at Wieringen,
       Holland 146, 202
Wizard 191, 192
Wobbelin 209, 211

Y

Young, Harold 168

ABOUT THE AUTHOR

Bob Gillette's entire professional career revolved around young people. For forty years, he was a public school educator. He was nationally recognized for his high school program OTO (Opportunities to Teach Ourselves) in Fairfield, Connecticut. For

The author celebrates the dedication of the Hyde Park Farm as a Virginia and National Historic Site after the story became known in his book *The Virginia Plan: William B. Thalhimer and a Rescue from Nazi Germany*. Burkeville, Virginia, April 21, 2013. *Courtesy of Michael Gillette.*

his innovations in experiential education, he was awarded the Mary Gresham Chair, a $300,000 grant by the New England Program for Teacher Education and the Department of Commerce. Among many recognitions for his teaching, he received the Harvard Teaching Prize. He has spoken and consulted nationally on educational topics. Simultaneously, he directed religious education programs and created curriculum in Jewish education. He is a graduate of Wesleyan University, earning a BA and an MAT, and he studied at the Hebrew Union College, the Reform Jewish rabbinical seminary. An avid canoe paddler, his first book written in retirement, *Paddling Prince Edward Island*, a Falcon Guide, was published in 2006. His second book, *The Virginia Plan: William B. Thalhimer and a Rescue from Nazi Germany*, was published in 2011 by The History Press.

Bob and his wife, Marsha, paddling partners for fifty-six years, live in Lynchburg, Virginia. They have enjoyed sharing the years of numerous book talks and research excursions. They are Connecticut Yankee transplants who enjoy discovering their new "southern Jewish roots." They have three sons and daughters-in-law, four granddaughters, a grand-cat and three grand-dogs.